SELFCARE
WELLCARE

SELFCARE
WELLCARE

KEITH W. SEHNERT, M.D.

AUGSBURG Publishing House • Minneapolis

SELFCARE/WELLCARE

Chapter 10, "The Selfcare Guide," is based on material that first appeared in *The Family Doctor's Health Tips* by Keith W. Sehnert, published in 1981 by Meadowbrook Press.

The information contained in this book is based on the knowledge and experience of the author and standard medical procedures adopted by lay groups and other professionals dealing in the areas of their experience. The contents of this book have been reviewed and checked for accuracy and appropriateness of application by other medical doctors. However, the author, reviewers, and publisher disclaim all responsibility arising from any adverse effects or results which occur or might occur as a result of the application of any of the information contained in this book. If you have questions or concerns about the appropriateness or application of the selfcare treatments described in this book, consult your health-care professional.

Scripture quotations unless otherwise noted are from the Holy Bible: New International Version. Copyright 1978 by the New York International Bible Society. Used by permission of Zondervan Bible Publishers.

Library of Congress Cataloging-in-Publication Data

Sehnert, Keith W.
  SELFCARE/WELLCARE.

  Bibliography: p.
  Includes index.
  1. Health. 2. Self-care, Health. 3. Mind and body.
I. Title.
RA776.S4525   1985   613   85-15622
ISBN 0-8066-2179-6
ISBN 0-8066-2180-X (pbk.)

Manufactured in the U.S.A.   APH 10-5645

1 2 3 4 5 6 7 8 9 0 1 2 3 4 5 6 7 8 9

Contents

Preface

In writing a book that discusses and describes the "hows" and "whys" of wellness and medical selfcare, an author such as myself better practice what he preaches. I can say in all objectivity that I practice these concepts and, indeed, have practiced them all my life. They are as much a part of me as my Henry Fonda-like face.

Wellness has been described as a mountain riddled with deep gorges, littered with giant boulders, and covered with dense forests. It is up such a mountain that individuals must climb—one step at a time—until they reach the sunny peak, see the blue skies, and experience that goal called high-level wellness.

The reality about such a climb is that in today's troubled times negative life-styles can present far too many deep gorges into which people can fall, economic conditions can roll giant boulders across our pathway of life, and unplanned circumstances can make us lose our way in the dense forests of change and stress. To counterbalance such forces, this book has been written to serve as a sourcebook for "mountain climbers," including many of the same quarter million readers who bought *Stress/Unstress* and found it a useful resource for themselves and the ones they love.

The names of persons whose health situations are profiled in this book are fictitious. While the profiles are drawn from actual cases, details have been changed to make the individuals unrecognizable.

Before we begin our hike up "Mount Wellness," I want to pay tribute to two fellow hikers who happen to be members of my family. Colleen, my wife and business manager, gets special thanks for her typing and many editorial suggestions in this book. My youngest daughter, Sarah, gets recognition for the many tactical duties she performed in getting this book out on time. I have appreciated her assistance. I'd also like to acknowledge the work of "forest ranger" and consulting editor, Ron Klug, who helped in a significant way and put out a few "brush fires" along the path.

With those acknowledgments in order, let us begin our hike up the "mountain."

CHAPTER ONE

Wellcare: Your Way to Health and Happiness

All of us would like to lead healthy, happy lives. We want to develop our gifts and use them in creative, satisfying ways. We want loving relationships. We want our lives to have purpose and meaning. We want to be all that we can be. We long for total wellness—physical, mental, and spiritual—and the way to total wellness is *wellcare*.

Wellcare: a way of life

Wellcare is a word I coined to combine the concepts of *wellness* and *stewardship*. In order to understand its significance, let us examine the two words that make it up. *Well* has several meanings, but in a medical sense it means, "in good health, sound in body, mind, and spirit" as in, "I'm feeling *well*, thank you." *Care* means "an object of concern or attention," as in, "Her child is her greatest care." Or *care* can mean "temporary keeping, for the benefit of, or until claimed by the owner" as in, "Address my mail *in care of* the American Embassy."

The Bible declares, "Your body is a temple of the Holy Spirit" (1 Cor. 6:19). If we learn to see our bodies as the temples of God, the words behind *wellcare* take on profound meaning. Your body, mind, and spirit can then be viewed as a National Historic Place, a rare book, a valuable work of art—all temporarily being kept by you with the responsibility to maintain them in good condition until they are claimed by the owner who is God. In that light the concept of *wellcare* becomes a total program, a way of life.

My concept of wellness grows out of my observation of the medical scene over the past decade. In America, social change seems to occur with movements. We had the civil rights movement, the women's movement, the consumer movement—now we have the wellness movement. Such movements bring with them needed reform, legislation, leaders, books, periodicals, and organizations.

The basis for the widespread interest in the wellness movement is an increasing appreciation for better nutrition, cleaner air, increased physical fitness, improved stress management, healthier lifestyles and environments, less costly medical care, and increased self-responsibility for health-care actions and decisions.

Building on the work of Dr. John W. Travis, I have developed an "Illness-Wellness Continuum" (see illustration on p. 11). The center of the scale shows absence of illness. Moving from the center towards the left shows a progressively worsening state of health. Moving to the right indicates an increasingly positive state of health, personal growth, and fulfillment of personal potential.

WELLCARE: YOUR WAY TO HEALTH AND HAPPINESS

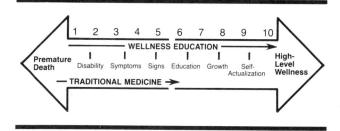

Most people, if asked how they feel at this moment, would respond, "OK," or "About average." That response would rate as 5 on my scale. If an individual just got out of the hospital or was recovering from the flu, that person would probably be a 2 or 3. Those who are running or keeping in shape with swimming, walking, watching their "nutritional Ps and Qs," and staying in touch with themselves and others might answer, "Great! Score me as a 9 or 10!"

If all the individuals were questioned in greater detail about how they feel, the responses probably would range from negative to positive:

Negative	**Positive**
Low energy/fatigue	High energy/stamina
Specific symptoms	Symptom free
Depressed	Sense of well-being
Insomnia	Sound sleep
Poor appetite	Good appetite
Apathy/dullness	Mental alertness
Frequent ills/colds	Few ills/colds
Tenseness	Calmness
Chemical abuse	No chemical abuse
Strained relationships	Sound relationships
Negative attitudes	Positive attitudes
Lack of new ideas	Creative

Overcoming the barriers to wellness

What are the causes of the problems and concerns that put people at a 2 or 3 on my wellness scale? What are some of the barriers that get in the way of high-level wellness? Based on my experiences as a family doctor, plus surveys and studies that have been conducted by others, I have prepared a table of sources of problems/concerns shown below.

Barriers to Wellness*

Nutritional Deficits	85%
Faulty Life-styles	80%
Life Adjustment/Emotional Concerns	70%
Allergic/Ecologic Factors	50%
Digestive/Absorptive Problems	20%
Infectious/Organic/Hereditary/ Traumatic Problems	15%

Problems associated with *nutritional deficits* are caused by diets that are inadequate in certain important minerals such as calcium; key vitamins including C, E, and B-complex; linoleic acid, and certain amino acids such as 1-cysteine and DL-methionine. The reasons these nutrients are inadequate may stem from deficits in dietary intake, poor absorption, and/or faulty food preparation and storage.

---

*The percentages noted represent general sources from the patients seeking my professional help. An individual could have more than one presenting problem when evaluated.

The patients who have *faulty life-styles* are those typical persons who have *too much* to eat, smoke, and drink, and who get too little sleep, exercise, and relaxation and recreation. For example:

Ken S., a 32-year-old male construction worker, was very overweight and knew it. He also smoked a lot—he liked his pipe and also smoked more than a pack of cigarettes each day. Ken's wife and his brother were after him to quit smoking and lose 30 pounds, but he said, "What the heck, I'm not that bad off. I'll do it *next year* when we move to that new construction site in Illinois."

Those with concerns described as *life adjustment/emotional* have recognized or unrecognized conditions related to family problems, personal relationships, jobs, and major life events that cause stress.

Allergic/ecologic factors afflict a large number of persons. These factors range all the way from the well-known hay fever caused by ragweed pollen to sensitivities to foods such as wheat and dairy products, drugs, and environmental factors such as petrochemical fumes, sensitivities to synthetic fibers, or reactions to building materials containing formaldehyde.

Digestive/absorptive problems frequently stem from deficits in the production of hydrochloric acid in the stomach and digestive enzymes in the liver, pancreas, and small intestine. Such deficits lead to a cascade of problems such as gaseousness, cramps, bad breath, foul-smelling bowel movements, and faulty absorption.

The final category, ***infectious/organic/hereditary/traumatic,*** is used to describe problems that can be related to a variety of common infections and to specific medical problems such as coronary heart disease, mitral valve insufficiency from rheumatic fever, cystic fibrosis, or diabetes mellitus, and, for example, a renal disorder resulting from injuries in a car accident or spinal cord damage from a skiing accident. These are the types of problems that are easily recognized by doctors during diagnostic work-ups.

These barriers to wellness are real, but to a very large extent most can be overcome. By putting into action the new understandings you gain from this book you can move to a higher level of wellness. You might become a 7 or an 8!

However, it may not be easy for you. There are some obvious limitations. You may come from a family in which all the males seem to have serious heart disease in their 40s and 50s. This is a hereditary condition. Or, you may have to function in a work environment that is far from optimal. There are some types of occupations—mining, for example—that carry a high risk of injury or death. Or, you may have a life-style that includes sedentary activity or smoking or abuse of alcohol. But remember, *you have the power to change.*

It is this possibility of change that is so exciting. New alternatives exist for health care. Employers are offering health promotion programs. There are new attitudes about wellness. New discoveries are being made about nutrition. The solutions for age-associated disorders like coronary heart disease, senility, and arthritis are coming.

The purpose behind writing this book was to help you learn about such changes and to help you develop a plan and aid you in implementing this plan. That's the meaning and basis of wellcare.

Test your wellness factor

Before you read on, take the following self-test to help you evaluate your health habits. After you have completed the test and have scored yourself, read on to find out what the results mean.

Please read the following statements and indicate if it has been your practice to:

1. get 7-8 hours of sleep per night.   Yes____No____

2. eat breakfast every morning.   Yes____No____

3. seldom eat between meals.   Yes____No____

4. keep within 10 pounds of your
   recommended "ideal weight."*   Yes____No____

5. exercise vigorously for 15-20 min-
   utes at least three times per week.   Yes____No____

6. not smoke.   Yes____No____

7. not drink more than two alcoholic
   beverages per day.   Yes____No____

Total score: Yes   No____

*Use the following formula to determine your "ideal" weight:
Women—100 + 5 pounds for each inch over 5 feet; *Men*—106 + 6 pounds for each inch over 5 feet. (If you exceed this rule by more than 10-20%, you are overweight. If you exceed it by more than 20% you are obese.)

This simple test has been called "The Seven Golden Rules of Good Health." The rules came out of the pioneering work of Lester Breslow and Nedra Belloc of the School of Public Health at U.C.L.A. Their studies showed significant and surprising relationships between common health practices and physical health status. Correlation was also found between the health practices and longevity.

What then do the results mean? Those who practiced most or all of the Golden Rules were healthier and lived longer than those who followed few of them. In your case, if you answered *yes* to six or seven of the questions the odds are you are likely to live a long and healthy life.

Using a survey of 6,928 adults in Alameda County, California, the UCLA researchers began their studies in 1970 and continued to track the health habits of these people over the next decade. Here is a brief summary of their findings:

Hours of sleep. It was found that eight hours of sleep was optimal for good health, seven hours followed closely, with nine hours or more significantly worse, and six hours or less least favorable.

Regularity of breakfast. People who ate breakfast regularly were consistently healthier than those who sometimes, rarely, or never ate breakfast.

Eating between meals. People who rarely or never ate between meals were healthier than those who snacked almost every day.

Weight in relationship to height. The average American is overweight—women by 15 to 30 pounds and men by 20 to 30 pounds—and is becoming more so each year. Saying it simply, people are overweight because they take in more calories than they burn up.

Physical activity. The more physically active, the healthier the population was found to be.

Alcoholic beverage consumption. Moderate drinkers or those who did not drink at all were significantly healthier than others.

Smokers. People who smoked were less healthy than those who did not. Furthermore, inhalers were less healthy than those who did not inhale, and there was a direct relationship between the number of cigarettes smoked and physical health.

Convergence of health practices. The more good health habits people practiced, the healthier they were. The physical health status of those who followed all good health practices was about the same as the physical status of those 30 years younger who followed few or none of the practices.

Life expectancy for a 45-year-old male was increased more than 11 years when the number of good health practices was increased from 0-3 to 6-7 health practices per year. The same change in health habits resulted in a seven year life expectancy increase for a 45-year-old female.

Clearly, life-style has a strong impact on our work, our energy levels, and our life expectancy. Recent reports have indicated that more than 90% of the ailments we suffer, we have brought upon ourselves. Thus the most significant impact on the health of Americans will not come from an increase in funds for acute care medicine, but from the impact of individual changes in life-style.

The remaining chapters of this book deal with how to improve personal habits and move toward greater total wellness. In them you will learn:

- how to use ancient wisdom and new research to live longer and more fully (Chapter 2);
- how to make sense out of the current controversy over nutrition and develop personal guidelines for healthy eating (Chapter 3);
- practical steps to help you handle stress and avoid burnout (Chapter 4);
- how to understand the vital role of spiritual health in total wellness (Chapter 5);
- how to get started on a personal fitness program that's right for you (Chapter 6);
- how to beat the high costs of health care and become a wiser user/buyer of health care services (Chapter 7);
- how to understand and evaluate the alternatives to orthodox medicine (Chapter 8);
- how to prepare for the changes that are coming in health care (Chapter 9); and
- how to practice selfcare and use the SOAP system to handle everyday illnesses, injuries, and emergencies without panic (Chapter 10).

CHAPTER TWO

Living Longer: Secrets Old and New

> Catherine C., 79, free-lance writer. The hobby she started 20 years ago became her vocation and Catherine has now written several books and a hundred or more articles. She attends Bible class and church on a regular basis and spends each Wednesday at a nursing home reading to the "old people."
>
> •
>
> Fred R., retired draftsman. Fred and his wife, Jenny, live on a small acreage and raise their own produce. After his retirement he took up oil painting, and he's now known as the Grandpa Moses of western Michigan. Jenny maintains an active correspondence with her six children and 12 grandchildren. She bowls regularly and sings in a local barbershop quartet.

People like Catherine and Fred and Jenny—and there are millions of them in the United States—are not only living longer, they are living active, healthy, creative, and exciting lives, filled with new learning and new challenges. With proper *wellcare*, you too can look forward to the blessings of a longer, healthier, active life.

Ancient secrets from the elders of the world

Gerontologists, medical specialists who study the process of aging, have long been interested in the elders who live in certain parts of the world: the Andean village of Vilcabamba, Ecuador, the republic of Abkhazia in the southern part of the Soviet Union, and the land of Hunza at the crossroads of Pakistan and Afghanistan.

Most scientists who have studied these "elders of the world" find stress-free environments with high social status for the aged. Each of the elderly persons lives with family and close relatives and has a strong sense of usefulness. Each has daily duties essential to the economic livelihood of the family, such as weeding the garden, feeding poultry, tending flocks, washing the laundry, weaving, caring for the children, and settling domestic disputes. All seemed to have a placid state of mind and emphasized the importance of being independent and free to do the things they enjoyed and wanted to do.

In such cultures the importance of married life is apparent. One of the most extensive studies was done by Professor G. E. Pitzkhelauri, a Soviet gerontologist, who found that, with few exceptions, only the married reach advanced age. He noted that women who had many children tended to live longer than those who were childless. The Russian scientist found that 44% of the women studied had four to six children and several had more than 20 children. He concluded that marriage and a regular sex life are very important to longevity.

Scientists also say that heredity plays a major role in longevity; very old individuals had parents who lived to be very old. Almost all elders studied in Hunza and the other two sites had at least one parent or sibling who had lived more than 100 years. In all these settings, because of the remoteness and mountainous terrain, the genetic strain has been kept "good" by preventing the introduction of "bad" genes from the outside. This observation about "good genes" has also been found in Norway (which has the greatest longevity of any western European nation) and may play a role in the long life of people in Minnesota, many of whom have Norwegian family roots. The Japanese gene pool has an effect on the longevity of the citizens of Hawaii. According to a recent report by the National Center for Health Statistics, Hawaii ranks #1 and Minnesota ranks #2 in life expectancy.

The Hunzans are Shiite Moslems, and their religious beliefs preclude the use of alcohol or drugs of any kind. It also fosters traditions in which male and female roles are clearly defined and interdependence between people and the environment is emphasized. The villagers in Ecuador are members of the Roman Catholic church and live in a culture that emphasizes strong family ties set by long tradition. There are several ethnic groups in the Caucasus area including Georgians, Russians, and Armenians. Here is mixed the religious heritages of Russian and Greek Orthodox, Roman Catholicism, plus Islam and Judaism. All have traditions that emphasize the importance of each individual in the community.

Wisdom from the elders of the world

If you were to summarize what can be learned from these elders in the far reaches of the world, it would be this:

- Eat simple fare for your diet with an emphasis on low protein, low fat, low sugar, and high bulk food that is rich in fruits and vegetables grown close to home.
- Develop an active physical life with lots of walking and vigorous work such as farming.
- Marry early in life and rear a large, closely-knit family.
- Maintain a strong sense of economic usefulness in your family and community and keep involved during your entire life.
- Develop your spiritual, philosophic, and religious values early in life and keep active in your church, synagogue, or religious organization.

New wisdom from the scientist's laboratory

While we can learn some secrets of a long, healthy life from elders of the world like the Hunzans, we in the United States also have new wisdom based on the most recent scientific research.

In the past few years doctors and scientists have learned more about what goes on inside the cells that make up human organs and tissues. This new knowledge has opened up the theory of free radical pathology. This theory holds great hope for those of us interested in longer, healthier lives.

Harry B. Demopoulos, a professor at New York University, has made discoveries about free radical pathology that are as profound and will have as much impact on medical care as the development of the germ theory a century ago. In the 19th century the work of Pasteur, Koch, and others led to the science of bacteriology, which helped create our modern treatments for infectious disease. Now, Demopoulos has proposed the concept that highly reactive molecules and molecular fragments called free radicals are present in the body and its tissues. They are constantly being formed and destroyed in the body as part of the process of homeostasis, the natural balance of the body. This balance is required by the body to maintain health in growth, repair, activity, rest, digestion, and excretion.

When free radicals get out of control, however, they help set the stage for diseases such as arteriosclerosis, dementia, arthritis, cancer, and other age-related diseases. These molecular particles are highly reactive and can bond quickly with other molecules. When a free radical reacts with another molecule it "can produce a cascade of free radicals in a multiplying effect." This effect can produce harm similar to the effects of X-ray and cosmic radiation. Uncontrolled free radicals of energy knock electrons out of orbit and create a cascade of free radicals in the surrounding tissues. This may lead to cancer or substantial changes within living tissues such as as atherosclerosis, inflammation, or cell death.

However, not all free radical reactions are dangerous. Many occur normally in the body and are necessary for health. Examples of normal functions include the detoxification process in which free radicals are involved in the breakdown of drugs, alcohol, artificial colorings, petrochemicals, and chemical fumes. There are thousands of other actions in antioxidant enzyme systems that help digest food, create hormones, and maintain homeostasis.

Elmer M. Cranton and James P. Frackelton described in a landmark paper about free radicals and chelation therapy *(Journal of Holistic Health,* Spring/Summer 1984) how healthy reactions are controlled by substances called antioxidants (Vitamins C and E are examples) which minimize the adverse effects of free radicals. The cascading effects are managed in a way somewhat similar to a controlled fire in a furnace, with the draft open just the right amount to warm the house, but not enough to allow the fire to get out of control and damage the furnace or burn the house down. Another analogy for such control might be the rods in a nuclear reactor. When they are adjusted properly, they prevent excess heat and even meltdown of the power station.

It is when free radicals cause a chain reaction and multiply in an uncontrolled way that the cells in the body are broken down. Such events start the onset of age-associated or degenerative disease.

Now how do all these chemical terms and free radicals pertain to you and your family? What can you do to help enzymes and antioxidants and reactions work for you? This is where your lifestyles, EDTA chelation therapy, and several other things you can control come into play.

EDTA (ethylene diamine tetraacetic acid) is an organic compound, a synthetic amino acid, that has powerful chelating or "grabbing power" and an affinity for calcium, lead, cadmium, iron, copper, aluminum, and other metals. EDTA is now known to *reduce the production of free radicals.* This is done by removing abnormal accumulations of trace metals that serve as accelerators (catalysts) and speed proliferation of free radicals. EDTA binds ionic metal catalysts, making them chemically inert and removing them from the body in the urine. This lowers radical formation to a certain threshold so that normal enzyme and body systems can keep the "fire in the furnace" from burning so hot that things are damaged at the cellular level. A naturally occurring form of chelation therapy is exercise, particularly aerobic exercise. When an individual does vigorous exercise, the skeletal muscles form lactic acid. This apparently produces cardiovascular benefits in part by its chelating effect. Another naturally occurring chelator is the citric acid found in fruits such as lemons and oranges. Therefore, both regular exercise and adequate fresh fruit in the diet, long known to be good health habits, also help keep down accumulations of free radicals and help maintain a healthy balance.

EDTA can also be given in three doses with certain vitamins and minerals in a 500 ml. intravenous solution. The therapy is given once or twice weekly. Each treatment lasts about four hours. The average number of treatments given is 25. (More details about chelation treatment can be obtained from the American Academy of Medical Preventics, 6151 W. Century Blvd., Los Angeles, CA 90045).

Assessing your longevity factor

One day a patient, Fred B., came into my office to talk about life-style. He knew about my interest in Hunza and said, "Now don't tell me about what they do in Hunza. The closest I will ever get to India is through the *National Geographic* on my coffee table. How do I start right here?"

With that, I handed him a copy of my "Medical Age Self-Test." "Finish this first," I said, "and then we can sit down together, evaluate the results, and decide on where to start."

Medical Age Self-Test

Directions: If uncertain, leave blank. Place scores (given in parentheses) on lines provided in the + or − columns. Total the + and − columns and subtract the lower number from the higher number to find the total (+ or −) for each section. Follow the instructions for calculating your medical age at the end of the appraisal.

1. Life-style Inventory   +   −

Disposition. Exceptionally good natured, easy going (−3); average (0); extremely tense and nervous most of time (+6).

Exercise. Physically active employment or sedentary job with well-planned exercise program (−12); sedentary with moderate regular exercise (0); sedentary work, no exercise program (+12).

Home environment. Unusually pleasant, better than average family life (−6); average (0); unusual tension, family strife common (+9).

Job satisfaction. Above average (−3); average (0); discontented (+6).

Exposure to air pollution. Substantial (+9).

Smoking habits. Nonsmoker (−6); occasional (0); moderate, regular smoking 20 cigarettes, 5 cigars, or 5 pipefuls (+12); heavy smoking 40 or more cigarettes daily (+24).

Alcohol habits. None or seldom (−6); moderate, with less than 12 oz. of or 2 beers or 5 oz. wine or 1¼ oz. hard liquor daily (+6); heavy, with more than above (+24).

Eating habits. Drink skim or low fat milk only (−3); eat much bulky food

SELFCARE/WELLCARE

(− 3); heavy meat (3 times a day) eater (+ 6); over 2 pats butter daily (+ 6); over 4 cups coffee/tea/cola daily (+ 6); usually add salt at table (+ 6).*

Auto driving. Regularly less than 20,000 miles annually and always wear seat belt (− 3); regularly less than 20,000 but belt not always worn (0); more than 20,000 (+ 12).   ____   ____

Drug habits. Use of cocaine, heroin, or street drugs (+ 36).   ____   ____

Subtotal   ____   ____

Part 1 total (+ or −)   ____   ____

2. Physical Inventory   +   −

Weight. "Ideal" weight at age 20 was _____. If current weight is more than 20% over that, score (+ 6) for each 20 pounds. If same as age 20, or less gain than 10 pounds (− 3).   ____   ____

Blood pressure. Under 40 years, if above 130/80 (+ 12); over 40 years, if above 140/90 (+ 12).   ____   ____

Cholesterol. Under 40 years, if above 220 (+ 6); over 40 years, if above 250 (+ 6).**   ____   ____

---

*The score is the sum total of all these food items.
**If you don't know your cholesterol leave score blank.

Heart murmur. Not an "innocent" type (+24).   ___   ___

Heart murmur with history of rheumatic fever. (+48).   ___   ___

Pneumonia. If bacterial pneumonia more than three times in life (+6).   ___   ___

Asthma. (+6).   ___   ___

Rectal polyps. (+6).   ___   ___

Diabetes. Adult onset type (+18).   ___   ___

Depressions. Severe, frequent (+12).   ___   ___

Regular* medical checkup. Complete (−12); partial (−6).   ___   ___

Regular* dental checkup. (−3).   ___   ___

Subtotal   ___   ___

Part 2 total (+ or −)   ___   ___

3. Family and Social History Inventory   +   −

Father. If alive and over 68 years, for each 5 years above 68 (−3); if   ___   ___

---

*"Regular" refers to *well* people who have thorough medical exams at a minimum according to this age/frequency: 60 and up, every year; 50-60, every 2 years; 40-50, every 3 years; 30-40, every 5 years; 25-30, as required for jobs, insurance, military, college, etc. More frequent medical checkups are recommended by other authorities. Dental exams: twice yearly.

alive and under 68 or dead after age 68 (0); if dead of medical causes (not accident) before 68 (+3).

Mother. If alive and over 73 years, for each 5 years above 73 (−3); if alive under 68 or dead after age 68 (0); if dead of medical causes (not accident) before 73 (+3).

Marital status. If married (0); unmarried and over 40 (+6).

Home location. Large city (+6); suburb (0); farm or small town (−3).

Subtotal	——	——
Part 3 total (+ or −)	——	——

4. For Women Only

	+	−
Family history of breast cancer in mother or sisters. (+6).	——	——
Examine breasts monthly. (−6).	——	——
Yearly breast exam by physician. (−6).	——	——
Pap smear yearly. (−6).	——	——
Subtotal	——	——
Part 4 total (+ or −)	——	——

Calculations

	+	−
1. Enter total from Part 1 (placed in appropriate column)	___	___
total from Part 2	___	___
total from Part 3	___	___
total from Part 4	___	___
Enter the totals of each column	___	___
2. Compute total (+ or −)		_____
3. Enter current age		_____
4. Divide total in line 2 by 12, and enter that (+ or −) figure		_____
5. Add or subtract above figure to/ from your current age to determine your medical age		_____

This questionnaire, along with your answers, can be a valuable reminder in assessing your life-style for optimal health. Use it as a daily check list—post it where you can see it every day.

Adapted from *How to Be Your Own Doctor, Sometimes* by Keith W. Sehnert, M.D. with Howard Eisenberg, Grosset & Dunlap, New York.

Fred finished the test and came up with a medical age of 69. "Well, Doc, maybe that's why my 'get-up-and-go' has got up and went!" He had exceeded his chronological age of 54 by 15 years!

Fred (who now seemed much more interested in life-styles than he had been 10 minutes earlier) sat down as I explained, "Such a test is only a rough guide, but provides some useful indicators. You are a typical middle-aged American male in that you are too sedentary, smoke cigarettes despite all the warnings, drink too much coffee, eat too much salt, are 20 pounds overweight, and live in a modern city with all its stress and pollution."

He noted philosophically, "Yeah, life American-style!"

"Don't look so discouraged," I said. "You've got a lot of things going for you. You have a good marriage. You like your work, and your company has a series of new health promotion programs that can help you get more exercise, improve your eating habits, and stop smoking. These things alone could help you lower your weight and blood pressure and knock off enough points from your score to bring you down to your chronological age. Then, with a little more fine tuning with what we know now about antioxidants, minerals, and improved eating and cooking habits, you will soon be feeling and looking a lot better."

I'm pleased to report that Fred did change his negative life-style, because when he saw me at church several months later, he gave me a friendly squeeze on my arm and whispered in my ear, "You should know that my 'get-up-and-go' has *come back* and I'm now *younger than my birthdate!*"

CHAPTER THREE

The Nutritional Controversies: Why All the Fuss?

Malnutrition is said to cause 50,000 preventable hospital deaths per year in the United States alone, while affecting another half million patients' recovery," reported *Forbes* magazine (April 9, 1984). Dr. Stanley J. Dudnick, a clinical professor of surgery at the University of Texas at Houston and one of the pioneers in the nutrition of hospitalized patients, said that over 30% of hospital patients are malnourished. "If you've lost 30% of your ideal body weight," Dudrick continued, "—which one-third of these people have—your chance of making it through an operation is about 5%."

Jack R., a 52-year-old furniture store owner, was admitted to the hospital. He had been ill for three months and eaten poorly so that when an operation was scheduled he was 20 pounds below his normal weight of 140. Although the surgery was "successful," Jack developed an infection and anemia. After eight weeks and 35 days in the Intensive Care Unit, he weighed only 100 pounds. His records showed that he had been given no vitamins or supplements except for a small dose of folic acid for a specific type of anemia. He received a low-salt diet, but most of the time could not eat and received daily IV fluids. On his 83rd day in the hospital, Jack developed a high fever and died. A consultant who later reviewed the case wrote this note: "The patient probably represents a classic case of hospital-staff-in-duced-protein-calorie malnutrition that resulted in terminal starvation."

How could this situation of nutritional neglect happen in one of our nation's leading hospitals? How could consultants in hematology, internal medicine, and vascular surgery overlook the nutritional problems suffered by this patient?

The case raises several more common questions about nutrition that many people have asked me:

1. Why do so many doctors have this mind-set against food supplements?
2. Can I get all I need for good nutrition by eating three "balanced" meals each day?
3. Why are many physicians negative about *Prevention* and similar magazines?
4. What is behind the controversary about Minimal Daily Requirements (MDR) and Recommended Daily Allowances (RDA)?*

---

*The term Minimal Daily Requirement (MDR) relates to a level of vitamin need that will result in illness if not available. A well-known example is that of Vitamin C. If the MDR of C is not met, then scurvy will result after a period of several weeks of deficient intake. The RDA is arbitrarily 50% higher than the MDR. They are not meant to be *optimal* intakes.

5. What are all those health food stores doing but hurting the "doctoring" business?
6. Is there a conspiracy by international cartels to push pharmaceuticals, at the expense of vitamins, for greater profits?

Why all the fuss?

I'll try to answer these questions as I understand them. My answers are based on my research as a former medical director for a Swiss pharmaceutical company, my work as a family doctor, and my experience with nutrition at Trinity Health Care, a holistic health center.

Much of the controversy surrounding nutrition boils down to whose beliefs are "correct," who holds the "most knowledge," who has published the most papers or books, and who is on the "left" or the "right" of the issue. As in all such controversies—political, religious, economic, medical—the truth is seldom on one side of the road or the other, but somewhere in between. Truth frequently needs the passage of time to arise from the dust of the immediate battle. It usually needs to leak out a bit at a time.

Then, let's look at "truth" in this nutritional controversy. There is an interesting special problem often not appreciated by the general public. When you are not trained in the scientific method, you do not realize that much of medical science is not *absolute fact*—but merely observations by a series of scientists. Two scientists can look at a glass that is 50% filled with water. One reports the glass is half *full*; the other observer notes that it is half *empty*. Both are right!

An example of such differences in observation occurred in a report by Michael W. Pariza of the University of Wisconsin in the *Journal of the American Medical Association* (251 [1984]: 1455-58). Pariza, commenting on how diet and nutrition might reduce the incidence of cancer, said, "Different experts looking at much the same epidemiologic and laboratory data, may react differently. However, what we are now learning is that the matter is bewilderingly complicated because the process of carcinogenesis is itself so complex and influenced in so many ways by our individual personal environments."

The man—or woman—on the street is puzzled when such scientific data say *different* things to different doctors about nutrition. In scientific medicine, clinical findings are often presented as "case reports." A doctor in Group A, which agrees with these findings, calls it a "good" study. Group B physicians may disagree and classify the same report as "anecdotal"—with the implication that the researcher should do better homework next time. Such differences make it more accurate to describe medicine as an art—not a science! This brings me to the questions that are frequently directed to me. Some experts will disagree with my answers, but they are the truth as I see it.

1. Why do so many doctors have this mindset against food supplements?

A friend once said, "People are *down* on things they are not up on!" This probably best explains why so many doctors are against food supplements and maintain that three meals provide balanced nutrition for most people. The reality is that most physicians have little training in nutrition because it has been given a low priority in medical schools. Now, with an increasingly knowledgeable citizenry and with several million patients "into nutrition," many doctors are reluctant to admit ignorance of the subject and so are "down" on it!

2. Can I get all I need for good nutrition by eating three "balanced" meals each day?

The problem with achieving adequate nutrition by eating three "balanced" meals a day is related to changes taking place in the soils of many farms, which, in turn, can change the nutritional content of our food. Soil scientists from states where truck gardens and citrus farms are located report that significant decreases in the amount of selenium, zinc, manganese, and molybdenum in the soil have occurred over the past 25 to 100 years. They have also found increases in dangerous heavy metals such as lead, mercury, and cadmium. The sources of such heavy metals are sewage wastes and sprays containing heavy metals that were once applied as fungicides for fruit. Other agricultural chemicals which cause soil changes by killing the normal soil bacteria come from herbicides (weed killers), insecticides, and nematocides (worm killers). Still other sources of soil pollution are auto exhaust fumes and substances put on streets and sidewalks to melt snow and ice. Whatever the source, the bottom line is that our soils have changed and the foods they grow are also changing.

3. Why are many physicians negative about Prevention and similar magazines?

Prevention was founded by J. I. Rodale, a successful businessman who became interested in organic gardening and better nutrition. He had personally been helped by improved nutrition and became a "true believer." As such, he had a religious fervor about vitamins and supplements and presented such viewpoints in the magazine. In the early years there were extravagant claims in the content and advertisements. It was not unusual to see an article about Vitamin C on one page and an ad for Vitamin C tablets on the opposite page. Perhaps for this reason many doctors were offended by the magazine.

Readers of today's *Prevention*, now edited by Robert Rodale, will find a more balanced layout and content. Now, boasting a circulation of 2.75 million readers, the publication has become a success and can afford to be more discriminating. Rodale has also taken on the role of helping mobilize not only nutrition-oriented readers but medical selfcare advocates with the establishment in 1983 of the People's Medical Society (now with 80,000 members).

4. What is behind the controversy about Minimal Daily Requirements (MDR) and Recommended Daily Allowances (RDA)?

Recently Dr. Arthur Leon of the University of Minnesota said that RDAs are "excessive for most people." At the same time, Earl Mindell, author of *Vitamin Bible*, said that most RDAs "are not meant to be optimal intakes, nor are they recommendations for an ideal diet. . . . Individuals vary by wide margins ... as far as I am concerned, the RDA ... [is] woefully inadequate." Those two statements express divergent opinions at the heart of the controversy.

Such disagreements began in 1974 when the U.S. Food and Drug Administration tried to make those formulations with doses greater than the RDA available *by prescription only*. The large pharmaceutical firms supported the FDA in this ruling because they knew their existing contacts with druggists would make them favored suppliers and, in turn, force some smaller manufacturers out of business.

This power play almost succeeded until an uproar from consumers, health food store owners, processors and distributors of vitamins and supplements, and various public-interest organizations deluged Congress with mail and phone calls. The response is alleged to have been the biggest outcry from the public over any issue except the Vietnam War.

The result of the furor was a political—not a scientific—decision to establish the RDA dosage at about 50% higher than MDR. For example, iodine was 0.1 mg. for MDR and became 0.15 mg. for RDA labeling. Veteran observers say that this clamor created today's health-food industry and brought a new respect by Congress for consumer rights.

The original scientific criteria for MDR levels came from discoveries that certain vitamins prevented or cured specific disease: Vitamin C for scurvy, Vitamin B1 for beriberi, etc. As we've learned more about these vitamins, it has been found that in addition to the *specific* actions, many have general actions on the function of the body's enzyme systems. These include formation of steroids, hormones, cleansing of free radical pathogens, and so on. A good example is Vitamin C. In addition to preventing scurvy, it also alters the cells of the mucous membranes of the nose and throat, affects the lining of blood vessels, lowers the level of blood cholesterol, changes osteoclasts and fibroblasts in bone and connective tissue, helps in the formation of adrenocorticoid hormones, and has other activities in the body.

Whenever you discuss vitamins, the issues of prevention as well as function are involved. A good analogy of that dual role might be the grease in your automobile's transmission system. It has at least two roles: (1) *prevention*—it prevents specific damage that would result from the friction of metal against metal in the transmission; and (2) *function*—it aids in the shifting of gears, acceleration, and performance.

Vitamin C also has at least two functions: (1) it prevents specific damage like that in scurvy; and (2) it aids the function and performance of the body in healing and other activities.

5. What are all these health food stores doing but hurting the "doctoring" business?

Today's doctors feel besieged on all sides. Due to Medicare and Medicaid regulations and other edicts, hospital administrators are putting all sorts of restrictions on physicians regarding admission and discharge procedures. Insurance companies tell them what they'll pay for and how much.

Health Maintenance Organizations (HMOs) and other prepaid groups advertise heavily and try to entice patients away from private doctors. Business corporations set up medical selfcare, health promotion, and wellness programs to improve the health status of their employees and reduce the number of visits to the doctor's office. Medical schools turn out more and more young doctors who compete with those already in practice. All sorts of professionals such as nurse practitioners, physicians assistants, nurse midwives, therapeutic nutritionists, massage therapists, acupuncturists, to name a few, are now setting up their own practices to compete with physicians.

Now add to the doctors' headaches a whole new set of competitors: 12,000 to 15,000 health food stores. Some Wall Street analysts predict that the two megatrends for the U.S. stock market are personal computers and health and nutrition businesses. Within these stores are owners and managers who tell their customers how to stay healthy and avoid going to the doctor. No wonder there is medical paranoia!

It's easy to see how many doctors become naysayers when the subject of nutrition comes up. In trying to protect their best interests, many doctors find little good to say about "health food nuts" and "vitamin freaks." They probably wish they would just go away!

6. Is there a conspiracy by international cartels to push pharmaceuticals at the expense of vitamins for greater profits?

If you had asked me that question a year ago, I would have said, "No. There may be a 'conspiracy' of ignorance or disinterest by the medical establishment (the American Medical Association, the Pharmaceutical Manufacturers Association, the American Hospital Association, and the major health insurance companies)—but if you mean that a group of high-level American, Swiss, and German big shots sit around a table in Zürich plotting plots and fixing prices—I don't think so."

However, in the last two years, several things have happened on a personal and professional level that have shaken my perhaps naive and trusting attitudes. As I got involved in studying and using nontraditional therapies, I found that the medical establishment looks with disfavor on practitioners who do not follow the flock. I found out how strongly they can react when someone threatens their economic livelihood and vested-interest concepts of right and wrong.

Your nutrition action plan

Now that you understand a bit more about all this fuss over nutrition, you might be asking, "Where does it all leave me? What am I to choose for my own family? How bad off am I?"

In 1981 the Pillsbury Company surveyed the eating habits of 20,000 patrons of the downtown Minneapolis Public Library. A computerized program was designed that asked people what they had eaten during a certain time. From this came the startling results shown on the next page.

I think we can assume from this survey and others that there are several problems with our eating habits. We tend to:

The Pillsbury Report

69%	Deficient in B-complex and iron (sources for these are whole grain breads and cereals).
54%	Adequate calories but deficient in Vitamin C and A (sources for these are fresh fruits and vegetables).
54%	Deficient in calcium, B1-12 and protein.
44%	Too *much* protein.
42%	Too *little* protein.
19%	Adequate nutrients but *too many* calories.
2%	"Smart eaters" with adequate nutrients and calories.

- eat too many calories;
- eat too much salt;
- eat too much protein;
- need more calcium;
- need more Vitamin C, A, and B-complex; and
- need more antioxidants and trace minerals.

Based on the Pillsbury study, recommendations from the Select Committee on Nutrition and Human Needs from the U.S. Senate Hearings (1977), knowledge about eating habits of healthy centenarians in Hunza and elsewhere, and recent discoveries about free radical pathology, I have developed advice that is based on several assumptions:

- Dietary histories, blood and allergy testing, and hair analysis often will be required to assess specific needs of an individual.

- Trace element supplementation should be under the guidance of a health-care professional knowledgeable in nutrition.
- Iron and copper should be supplemented only to treat deficiency states.
- Sustained weight loss is possible only through a combination of fewer calories and regular aerobic exercise.

My general advice I call Sehnert's Secret Seven:

1. Greatly increase consumption of fiber-rich fruits (eating apples, oranges, and so on *whole*, not juiced), vegetables and nuts (using beans, peas, and fresh, whole, unheated nuts as major sources of proteins).
2. Greatly decrease consumption of fats and oils, including salad and cooking oils. Avoid all fried foods and use low-fat (1% or skim) instead of whole milk (remembering that fats, especially those containing extracted polyunsaturated fats, are the leading sources of pathological free radicals).
3. Increase consumption of poultry and fish (discarding poultry skin before eating) and decrease use of red meat (limiting it to lean, well-trimmed beef, pork, and lamb, three or four ounces every other day, and making sure it is not charred or overcooked).
4. Ensure intake of supplemental vitamins and antioxidants such as E, C, B-complex, B-12, pantothenate, PABA, beta carotene, and glutathione.
5. Ensure intake of minerals and trace elements such as zinc, magnesium, selenium, manganese,

and chromium in the form of supplements. (*Avoid* iron and copper unless known to be deficient by serum ferritin test for iron and hair or blood analysis for copper. This may be whole blood or erythrocyte copper. I take a basic multiple supplement *without* copper and iron.)

6. Greatly decrease consumption of refined and processed carbohydrates such as white sugar, white flour, and white rice (prominent ingredients of junk or processed foods)

7. Decrease consumption of salt and foods high in salt content and add no salt at the table.

These Secret Seven are based on this rule of thumb: the quality of the *food cell* creates the nutritional quality of the food. With this concept, then, the less processing or preparing or heating that is done to the fresh cell (of the plant or animal that provided the food), the higher the nutritional content of that food. For example, eating fruit whole is better than juicing it. Preparing an egg by poaching it or soft boiling it is better than scrambling it. Making bread from whole wheat flour is better than preparing it with white, bleached flour. Ordering steak that is "rare" is better than requesting "well done."

Now, you, of course, have another option. You can go to Hunza, and eat and live the way they do, and you can skip the vitamins and supplements. But if you can't afford the airfare to Pakistan, then you'd be smart to follow my advice!

CHAPTER FOUR

Stress and Life in the Fast Lane

> Stephanie S., 42 years old, business administrator and mother of three teenage daughters. She has found that her work as an office manager is increasingly time consuming. Recently she had to cancel several after-school events with Ann, her eldest girl, who stated angrily, "You care more about work than you do about me!" Stephanie tries to do errands over her lunch hour and shops for groceries on the way home from work, but clearly her home life is being disrupted more and more. She confided, "Life in the fast lane is getting to me. I've lost complete control of my life!"

How do you gain control? When you travel down the "Highway of Life" in the fast lane, are you in any danger? What are the causes and casualties of stress? How does your body "talk" to you when stress is heavy enough to cause medical troubles? What are the tips for controlling stress? Read on!

The causes and casualties of stress

The major source of stress is change, especially rapid change. Changes in your job, in your role as a man, woman, parent, or citizen; changes in your sleep, in your diet, in your exercise habits; changes in your family, friends, social, or community activities; changes in the noise level, intensity of lighting, or quality of the air you breathe; even changes in the air or barometric pressure can trigger a stress reaction.

When such changes occur, your body has to adjust in many ways. A good example is that of changes in air pressure as you come down from a mountain or land in an airplane. Your ears pop. Your breathing rate changes. There are changes in your blood pressure. Your body adjusts to a different situation.

The late Hans Selye, who has been called the "Father of Stress Studies," gave this definition about such changes: "Stress is the non-specific response of the body to any demand made upon it." In his book *The Stress of Life* (McGraw-Hill, 1976), Selye pointed out some common misconceptions about stress.

What stress *is:*

- Stress is the wear and tear caused by life.
- Stress is the mobilization of the body's defenses that allow human beings to adapt to hostile or threatening events.
- Stress is dangerous when it is unduly prolonged, comes too often, or concentrates on one particular organ of the body.

What stress *isn't:*

- Stress isn't an entirely bad event or negative occurrence.
- Stress isn't nervous tension.
- Stress isn't the discharge of hormones from the adrenal glands.

Dr. Kenneth R. Pelletier, author of *Mind as Healer, Mind as Slayer,* has described contemporary stress in terms of "excited" and "relaxed." Here are three case histories based on Pelletier's concept:

Case 1. *"A Few Minutes of Stress in Traffic"*

1. George B. is ready to go to work. He has had a good night's sleep and his body is at its baseline (or relaxed) state. George has a nourishing breakfast, kisses his wife good-bye and leaves home to drive to work.

2. After he enters the freeway his car is nearly hit by a large truck. The near accident scares him. His heart seems to flip-flop for a few minutes. He is very tense.

3. Fifteen minutes later he leaves the heavy traffic of the freeway and enters the quiet street near his office.

4. By the time he enters his office, he has settled down and is ready to start his work.

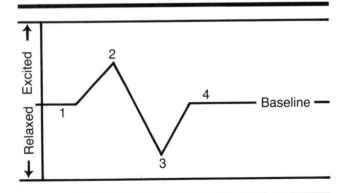

Case 2. "A Bad Day at Home"

1. Mary F. just sent her children out the front door to catch the school bus and now they are back telling her they missed the bus!

2. Back home after driving them to school, she finds her washing machine has leaked water all over the floor, and she has to call someone to repair it.

3. After cleaning up the mess, Mary gets a call from the school principal saying her son has fallen off the swing and is at the hospital and needs stitches.

4. When bedtime comes, she is so upset by the day's events she has difficulty falling asleep.

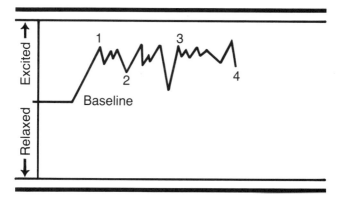

Case 3. "A Year of Trouble with a Capital T"

1. Bud H. heard rumors that his company is in danger of closing down because of poor business.

2. After weeks of uncertainty the rumors are confirmed and all employees are dismissed.

3. Bud gets a new job in Houston and the family moves. They can't sell their old home but have to buy a new house. Bud's kids and wife don't like Texas.

4. After his brother's sudden death on the family farm, Bud settles the estate, and returns to Houston in a depressed, fatigued state.

5. Bud ends up in the hospital for two weeks with a "mild heart attack."

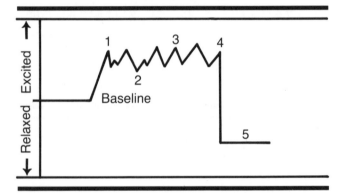

How does your body "talk" to you?

In each of these case studies, the individuals had experienced stressful situations. What had happened to their bodies? How had their bodies "talked" through symptoms? What can you learn about yourself by studying the things that happened to George, Mary, and Bud?

Case 1. George's sensation of a "flip-flop" of his heart was what doctors call "skipped beats" or "extra systoles." If George had been strapped up for an electrocardiogram, it might have shown an irregular series of QRS waves instead of a normal, clocklike rhythm. He would have also had an increased heart rate from its baseline rate of 70 to 100 or more beats per minute, and his blood pressure would have been higher.

Case 2. Had you been able to study Mary's responses on that "bad day" at home, you would have found more than the insomnia at bedtime. By the time she cleaned up after the repair had been made on the washing machine, there was a tightness in her shoulder muscles that made her stop for a few minutes and rub her neck vigorously. Eventually this tenseness developed into intense neck pain. By the time she got home from the emergency room, she also had a splitting headache.

Case 3. · Bud's heart attack was the final blow to his body after a year of "Trouble with a capital T." He first experienced the angina (chest pain) when he was told he would get no severence pay from the company even though he had worked there for 15 years. He had more pain plus severe mental depression before he finally got a new job in Texas. The death of his brother and all the turmoil that followed was the final blow that led him to the heart attack and put him in the hospital.

In each situation, the common bond was *change* that altered the normal balance inside the body:

In Case 1, the near accident heightened George's reflexes, increased his visual and hearing skills, got his juices flowing. These responses helped him survive. However, some of the "juices," in this case adrenaline from his adrenal glands, caused the normal pacemakers of his heart to be "knocked out of sync" for a few moments.

In Case 2, Mary's muscles in her neck tightened in order to do the extra work needed in driving the car to school, cleaning up the water and soap suds, and rushing to the hospital. She was on "battle alert" for a while, but because she tends to be a hard-driving, perfectionist homemaker and parent, this alert went into overdrive and stayed all day—and part of the night!

In Case 3, Bud found that years of physical neglect had made him prone to a heart attack. He smoked, was overweight, and out of shape. His eating habits were atrocious. So when the turmoil of job loss, relocation, and grief over his brother's death were added up, his narrowed coronary blood supply, elevated blood pressure, and high serum cholesterol led to the heart attack.

Symptoms follow the altered function of a part of the body. I want you to try two simulations to demonstrate how your body can talk. Put the book down and follow these simple directions:

Simulation #1
- Raise your right hand and arm straight above your head.
- Open and close your fist as fast as possible while counting.
- Count to 60 and then clench your fist as firmly as possible.
- Drop your arm and lay your hand (palm up) on your lap.

- Examine the color of the skin of your palm.
- Now ask yourself these questions: Did you have a pale palm that turned pink? Was there a tingling sensation in your palm? Was there aching in the shoulder or upper arm? Was there distress in the hand and wrist?

Simulation #2

- Clamp your nose tightly between your thumb and index finger.
- Open your mouth and breathe through your mouth.
- Take 12 deep breaths over an interval of 30 seconds.
- Now ask yourself these questions: Did you have a dry mouth? Did you get light-headed or dizzy? Did you cough?

The common bond that George, Mary, Bud, and you experienced was that of symptoms (body talk) produced by altering normal functions of your body. When, for example, you plug the nose with your fingers—or have a cold virus congesting your nose—you alter the normal moisturizing, warming functions of the nose. You get a dry mouth and cough because your vocal cords are no longer protected with a moist blanket of mucous. They have become dried out, and your voice turns raspy or hoarse. The fist-clenching exercise simulated the aches and pains associated with soreness from overly strenuous sports or work activity. You may have noticed a sore wrist, stiff shoulders, or aching fingers—all symptoms that result from a disruption of the normal blood flow to the hand and arm.

In addition to the physical symptoms observed in the three case studies, there can be mental or psychological symptoms. These happen when a person is subjected to stress overload for long periods of time. Bud experienced these:

- Decision making became difficult. ("I couldn't even decide which tie to wear.")
- Excessive day dreaming about getting away from it all. ("I thought a lot about our family cabin in the lake country.")
- Increased use of cigarettes and/or alcohol. ("My cigarette consumption went from one to two packs a day.")
- Worry about trivial things. ("Worry? Man, I worried about the dumbest things.")
- Sudden outbursts of temper/hostility. ("I sure had a short fuse.")
- Mistrust of friends and family. ("My paranoia was awful those days!")

When is stress heavy enough to cause medical troubles?

When people are subjected to stressful times over a period of weeks or months, many of them end up seeking some sort of professional help. They may consult with family doctors, nurses, counselors, pastors, psychologists, or a variety of other health professionals. As part of the interview, the professional sorts through the history and findings to establish a problem list. Common problems found that are related to stress include:

- sleep disorders (insomnia)
- high blood pressure (hypertension)

STRESS AND LIFE IN THE FAST LANE

- stomach hyperacidity and pain
- heart palpitations (cardiac arrythmia)
- nervousness (anxiety states)
- irritability

One of the reasons that people experience stress is that their lives become more complex, and as they try to do more things each week, they tend to lose control. Studies show that work consumes as much time as it did a generation ago—but the travel, the getting there and back, takes *more* time. It also takes more time for shopping, for maintenance of household equipment, and repairing our automobiles. As these nicks occur in our daily schedules, we have *less* time for family events, recreation, going to church, reflection, and just plain thinking.

We also have less time for doing a job right, whether it consists of typing a letter, baking some bread, or even assembling a new car. Herein develops another source of stress. We are less often able to take pride in our jobs. This conflict bothers many people who take pride in doing their jobs right. As our traditions of quality in work are lost, we feel guilty. Here's an example of what that can mean:

> **Jennifer C. is a middle-aged legal secretary. She had been a full-time homemaker until her youngest son entered junior high last fall. She then had the opportunity to work outside her home with one of the largest law firms in town. Her husband Dick called it a real "plush**

job," and everyone in the family pitched in to "help mom" do the housework while she worked at the office. All went well for six months. Then Jenny found these problems developing:

1. She didn't have the energy to help with her son's homework when he asked her. "Although I'm sharp at math, I couldn't even add straight," Jenny said with an apology.
2. Known for her quality baking and cooking, she found there was no longer time to bake bread or even her favorite casseroles. "It was fast foods and microwave specials four nights this week," Jenny said.
3. Her husband felt slighted when she no longer had time to critique his speeches and sales presentations.

Then one night she exploded with emotion. "I burned my son's shirt while watching TV, phoning my sister, and making my shopping list— all at the same time. That was the straw that broke this camel's back. I wasn't doing anything well! I cried for 10 minutes."

Jenny had skimped on her down time. She had all of her regular duties, but less time for eating, sleeping, socializing with friends and family, and time for her church and hobbies. She was unable to fulfill her role as "Super Mom"—and felt guilty about it.

Over 80% of us feel stress in our daily living these days. The General Mills survey, *American Family Report, Family Health in an Era of Stress* (done before the turmoil of the recession of 1980-82), found 41% of those surveyed felt a *strong* need to reduce stress in their daily lives. Another 41% felt *some* need to reduce stress. Not all of these persons could run to get professional help. That route is too expensive for many and ineffective for many others. What did they do? Some got help from friends and family. Others read books and went to classes.

What are some ways they learned to control the intensity of the symptoms and prevent others?

In my book, *Stress/Unstress* (Minneapolis: Augsburg, 1981), I provided a variety of methods for stress management. Here is a short summary of my advice:

1. Increase understanding of stress so that you can prevent much of it.
2. Identify early warning signals by "listening to your body" in a careful manner.
3. Do not use alcohol or tranquilizers as solutions.
4. Learn the five ways to control stress listed below.

Before I give some brief details about the five ways to use in the management of stress, I offer some words of caution. Americans like to have simple solutions for complex problems. When it comes to stress, many of you think of such solutions: "Take a 'stress tablet' with Vitamin C"; "Get a good workout once a week." Unfortunately, it's not that simple. The management of stress requires the concerted, whole-person approach that I will briefly describe now.

The five ways to control stress

1. Change your work and social environment.

The majority of people spend eight or more hours per day in a work place and another 10-12 in their home, apartment, or "social environment." If stress is getting to you, improve the conditions on the job and at home as much as possible. Control the noise, light, work station, and quality of air that will help you to be productive on the job. Minimize distress in family and social relationships and seek healthy recreation and quiet time for recovery from work stresses.

2. Understand your emotions.

Most of us find it easy to blame situations, people, and things "out there" for making us angry, sad, or distressed. Yet, it is not the *outside* things that cause us stress. It is our *inside* perceptions of what has happened that causes emotional turmoil.

It is important to understand your "Emotional ABCs." These provide the basis for understanding and changing one's emotions:

A—*Activating Event.* This means that an event stimulates one of your five senses (e.g., a sound you *hear*, a sight you *see*, the smoke you *smell*). These sensations trigger within your brain an informational or protective response.

B—*Belief System.* This system is composed of the entire matrix of one's religious, ethical, educational, and personal understandings. Some have attitudes of love, forgiveness, faith, hope, and charity that help them behave in a certain way. Others have attitudes of fear, hopelessness, and greed to govern their behaviors.

C—*Consequences (Emotional Responses).* Once the event has been filtered and evaluated, in a fraction of a second, your gut (or emotional) feelings—positive, negative, or neutral—are experienced. They may be felt as joy, depression, excitement, fear, or whatever. In gaining emotional control over some negative events, an individual may never experience positive feelings about the circumstances, but the emotions can at least be shifted from negative to neutral.

3. Learn unstress remedies.

When stress ties you in knots or events occur over which you have little control, and if you feel irritable and anxious and your body is talking to you, institute some safe and sane remedies such as stretching, visualizing, singing, or laughing. Unstress remedies have several common characteristics: deep breathing, muscle stretching, and mind centering. They help break the hold of the overactivated sympathetic portion of your autonomic nervous system. Most of the success of biofeedback is based on gaining insight in how to maintain control of such overactive sympathetics through various techniques.

4. Take care of your body.

You can manage stress more effectively when you are properly fed, well rested, and physically fit. Individuals who follow a wise nutritional program (see Chapter 3), adhere to the "Seven Golden Rules of Good Health" (see Chapter 1), and follow a regular fitness program (see Chapter 6) will cope more effectively with events during stressful times.

5. Provide for your spiritual needs.

Any stress management program will fail unless there is an enhancement of spiritual resources. Religion, worship, prayer, and meditation are integral parts of such a program. An individual is "whole" only if body, mind, and *spirit* are nourished. In our secular world it is much easier to groom, clothe, and feed our bodies than it is to groom, clothe, and feed our spirits. Such care is the work of churches, synagogues, and other religious organizations. It is also, of course, the work of individuals, friends, and families (see Chapter 5).

Life in the fast lane

Up until now I have been talking about how stress *affects* and *afflicts* individuals. How does

STRESS AND LIFE IN THE FAST LANE

life in this fast lane affect large numbers of individuals—such as everyone in a city or even all those in a state? Where is life in the fast lane the fastest? How does your state rate in the "Stress Sweepstakes?"

A recent study by three scientists helped shed light on this aspect of stress-at-large. Murray Straus, Arnold Linsky, and John Colby, sociologists at the University of New Hampshire, studied 15 stress indicators and concluded that the most stressful was Nevada. Alaska came out second, and high-growth western states such as California, Oregon, and Washington finished in the "Big Five." You can check how your state finished in the listing on p. 62.

The states with the *least* stress were these five midwestern states: Wisconsin, North Dakota, South Dakota, Iowa—and the winner of the Unstress Bowl is Nebraska. These states are all known for their stability. They are farm states and incorporate many of the values of rural family life with common roots in ethics, education, race, and religious backgrounds.

The analyses in this state-by-state study were based on factors ranging from the number of business failures to the number of divorces and high-school dropouts. Other factors used included indicators such as the number of people moving into a state and the rate of housing construction. These may seem like things that make the local Chamber of Commerce shout with glee because it means their towns and cities are prospering and growing. However, with such data often come some stress

SELFCARE/WELLCARE

1/Nevada	26/North Carolina
2/Alaska	27/Texas
3/Georgia	28/New Mexico
4/Washington	29/Arkansas
5/Oregon	30/Pennsylvania
6/Alabama	31/West Virginia
7/California	32/Missouri
8/Mississippi	33/Kansas
9/Arizona	34/Hawaii
10/Tennessee	35/Indiana
11/Colorado	36/Rhode Island
12/Oklahoma	37/Connecticut
13/South Carolina	38/Maine
14/Florida	39/Wyoming
15/Michigan	40/Vermont
16/New York	41/Massachusetts
17/Illinois	42/Montana
18/Idaho	43/Minnesota
19/Virginia	44/Utah
20/Kentucky	45/New Hampshire
21/Ohio	46/Wisconsin
22/Louisiana	47/North Dakota
23/Delaware	48/South Dakota
24/Maryland	49/Iowa
25/New Jersey	50/Nebraska

Figures used apply to residents of the states, not tourists. Calculations were based on 1976 statistics for 15 stress-related indicators; this was the last year for which data from all states were available when the study began four years ago. Source: *The Minneapolis Star and Tribune*, April 1, 1984.

penalties, because they represent significant change and many adjustments for individuals, families, companies, communities, and states.

The 15 indicators chosen by the scientists were:

1. High-school dropout rate
2. Number of illegitimate births
3. Divorce rate
4. Residents who had lived in the state fewer than five years
5. New welfare recipients
6. Number of business failures
7. Unemployment claims
8. People on strike
9. Bankruptcy claims
10. Mortgage foreclosures
11. Abortion rate
12. Fetal mortality
13. Infant deaths
14. Housing construction starts
15. Disaster assistance payments

Straus and his co-workers were interested in learning how these factors cumulatively affect crime rates, violence, physical health, mental health, and alcoholism. Factors such as suicide and illness rates were not included because they are more often the *result* of stress than the cause.

High-growth states such as Nevada have a "go-go" atmosphere, but high-growth communities in a state often experience gaps in needs for schools, roads, sewers, and community services. These in turn make for crowding, poor maintenance, shortages, and inadequate coverages—all of which can provide stressful situations for a city. Rapid growth also means that when people buy a new home—probably at a cost higher than the buyers expected to pay—there are financial strains on personal bank accounts. For example, a survey in 1984 by the United States League of Savings Institutions found that residents of Los Angeles and its suburbs faced the highest housing prices in the country—about 72% higher than the median price paid in a small midwestern town or rural area.

Although life in the city is often more hectic than that in the country, don't think for a minute that rural life is serene these days. An acquaintance of mine told me that this spring five of his lifelong friends were forced to have farm auctions. Since then, two have had heart attacks and a third has developed bleeding ulcers.

Many uprooted farm people have experienced ailments such as alcoholism, depression, and suicide. The economic and psychological turmoil surrounding farming and agribusiness is taking a great toll on the families of rural America.

In the final analysis the places we choose offer us a trade-off between benefits and headaches. If you choose to live in states that are undergoing rapid growth and social change, you are likely to find a more stressful environment. But one word of caution—don't move to the country to escape stress. You'll find it there, too!

Controlling stress through love and laughter

In *Stress/Unstress* I devoted many chapters to helping the reader understand stress enough to prevent much of it and providing methods to handle it when it caught up with people for reasons beyond their control.

STRESS AND LIFE IN THE FAST LANE

I would like to present here another method of stress control that I find is not only useful, but essential in handling stress—laughter. It is a tool people should use on a regular basis. Some of my thoughts about this were gained at a meeting entitled "The Healing Power of Love and Laughter: The Second Annual Holistic Medicine Conference," where several speakers gave scientific and clinical evidence about how laughter is helpful in controlling stress.

Norman Cousins reported on work from U.C.L.A. about "positive emotions" giving "positive biochemistry" and that laughter changes the biochemistry to the positive side. Cousins, in his book, *Anatomy of an Illness as Perceived by the Patient* (Bantam, 1981), used laughter as a resource in recovering from an arthritic type of stress-related illness. Through the use of reruns of the television series, "Candid Camera," and Marx Brothers movies, he found that laughter helped his formerly elevated erythrocyte sedimentation rate (sed rate) return to normal levels and he was able to increase his mobility through walking and moving around. He commented that rather than considering the brain just a "computer" (processor of information), it should be considered also an "apothecary" (manufacturer of hundreds of chemical agents and messengers). Cousins said that much of the damage from stressful situations occurs when fear, anger, depression, and negative emotions "slow down or even stop the apothecary."

An internationally prominent cancer specialist from Fort Worth, Texas, Dr. O. Carol Simonton, noted the close link between stress, depression, fear, and poor self-image and the development of various malignancies. He reported that the body knows how to heal itself—if given a chance. He observed, "When you cut your finger—you expect it to heal and it does. When you are frightened by cancer, fear can block the normal healing process and often does." Simonton uses visualization, games, play, and laughter to aid patients in recovery from cancer.

The discovery that laughter is therapeutic doesn't come as a surprise to many people who have observed: "A good laugh makes you feel good all over!" "The tension is often broken by a joke or wisecrack and I feel better afterward." "You can't laugh and worry at the same time!"

I use this laughter therapy as an antidote for tension. When I'm under a heavy load of stress, I try to make time for old TV favorites such as "M*A*S*H" or "Happy Days." Another method I like is to visit or telephone a friend who will tell me a good joke or give me a smile.

Some final thoughts about tension and stress

One night my wife, Colleen, and I were entertaining Richard Miles as our guest for dinner at our home. Miles, from San Francisco, is designer and former director of the graduate program in clinical holistic health education at John F. Kennedy University in Orinda, California, and a consultant for wellness and health promotion programs. We talked about stress and tension. Miles said, "As a matter of word origins, tension more accurately means *an imbalance of muscular forces* from *internal*, not external sources. I have developed a soliloquy for my class to show how key words relate to tension."

"WHEEL OF TENSION"

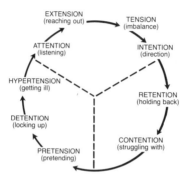

TENSION creates an imbalance within the body; INTENTION refers to the direction of desired movement; RETENTION is a holding back of the body's intention to complete that movement. CONTENTION involves struggling with or living with retention as a daily course of events.

Miles then noted that contending with tension without understanding it eventually drives the system to certain reflexive actions.

PRETENSION involves pretending the tension does not exist; DETENTION means locking up tensions without resolution; HYPERTENSION occurs when the body, after being on constant alert, resets its regulators at a "higher" level.

In addition to hypertension, other ailments including fatigue, headaches, back pain, and a variety of chronic disorders can develop.

ATTENTION, or alertness by listening to the body's signals, helps set the stage for recovery; EXTENSION, which means reaching out, is a positive action that helps release the inner tension.

Miles concluded his soliloquy by commenting that when an individual fails to understand tension and internalizes it, the body's capacity to seek balance and regulate normal functions fails and chronic disease begins.

As I watched Miles finish his sketch of the "Wheel of Tension" on a paper napkin, I thought about the fact that Christians, when confronted with stress, must remember "who's in charge."

Much of the turmoil associated with stressful situations comes from feeling out of control. Events happen that we don't like and didn't plan for and they send us off in different directions, which only adds to our distress. It is in such circumstances that we need that enduring resource for stress control—prayer.

Imprinted on a prominent place in the Sehnert kitchen is this favorite Bible verse: "Trust in the Lord with all your heart and lean not on your own understanding" (Prov. 3:5). This is age-old advice that still works. Use it.

CHAPTER FIVE

The Mind-Body-Spirit Connection

O ne of the most significant medical developments in the United States in the last decade has been the development of the *holistic* health movement. An increasing number of doctors now realize that there are medical as well as religious reasons for considering the spiritual health of their patients. The term *holistic* has the same word roots as *holy* or *sacred* as well as the mathematical meaning of being the sum of its parts. A holistic or wholistic health center, then, provides services that link spirit, mind, and body. Philosophically many holistic health practitioners believe the whole is *more* than the sum of the parts because of the enhancement of each on the others.

Much of the current interest in the field of holistic health came from work in 1956 by Granger Westberg, a hospital chaplain who developed his concept of health care first in Ohio and later in Illinois where he became the first clergyman to be appointed to the faculty of the University of Chicago Medical School. Westberg observed that the human body functions *best* when individuals receive and reflect attitudes of love, gratitude, and forgiveness—all spiritual qualities. He also noted that the body functions *worst* when there are attitudes of hate, anger, and envy—and a void of spiritual values. His studies showed that persons who had strong spiritual values seemed to weather surgery, physical ills, and injuries more successfully than individuals without such resources.

Westberg's work was not done in a vacuum; many related events were happening in America at the time. Why then, did the medical profession have to wait for a chaplain to make such a discovery? Some of the reasons go back as far as the time of Sir Isaac Newton, 250 years ago. Newton is known as the father of modern physics, but he was also a leader in the Age of Enlightenment and made a profound impact on the thinking of many philosophers, teachers, and academicians. Newton described the body as a machine with parts such as bars (arms), pulleys (muscles, tendons, joints), and a pump (heart). Interestingly, the mechanistic concepts he voiced over two centuries ago continued down to present times with my experiences in school. When I was a student at the University of South Dakota and later at Case Western Reserve University, I was taught a "parts philosophy." I learned about the stomach (from gastroenterologists), lungs (from lung specialists), the heart (from cardiologists), bones (from orthopedic surgeons), and the mind (from psychiatrists).

In the clinics and hospital wards I learned the body is owned by a person called a "patient" (who was perceived by our teachers as someone who didn't have much sense), who was referred to the university hospital by an "LMD" (an abbreviation for local medical doctor—who also didn't have very much sense or else the doctor would be working at the medical school). The job, then, of the elite "parts specialists" (the professors at the medical school) was to find out what ailed the patient and determine what surgery or pills should be used to get the parts working again.

There was no one in charge of the part called "the spirit," and for that reason we must go back even further into history to search out the reasons for that significant omission.

Until the 15th century, medical care in Europe and parts of the Middle East was closely connected with the Christian church. Hospitals that were staffed and built by individuals in Catholic nursing orders provided a whole-person ministry to the patients and their families. During the 16th century, however, a dramatic change occurred. A part of the Protestant Reformation included zealots who said, "If Rome is *for* it, we're *against* it!" This thinking produced unexpected events. In one area of England, for example, nearly 100 hospitals, built and run by nursing sisters for many decades, were systematically torn down, stone by stone, and carted away—leaving nothing behind but holes.

For the next 400 years whole-person health became fragmented, but the various turfs clearly defined. The *physicians* took care of the *body*, and the *preachers* took care of the *soul*. It wasn't until the 1950s that formal healing ministries became established. Healing services, with much help from radio and television broadcasting, soon spread across the country. Direct healing of a spiritual nature became more widely accepted. That acceptance, accompanied by the rise of pastoral counseling, the ecumenical Clinical Pastoral Education programs for chaplains, and the charismatic movement have helped holistic health come into the mainstream.

Maybe I should say "almost mainstream" because the word *holistic* has been usurped—some say even prostituted—by nontraditional practitioners and even advertising people. An example of such semantic gymnastics occurred during a recent trip to Hollywood for a TV appearance. I was driving down Sunset Boulevard when I noticed this message on a service station billboard: "Today Only. Holistic Car Wash!" In spite of society's increasing familiarity with the word, *holistic* still has a way to go before it has everyday application for most health-care professionals.

Some reflections on spiritual nourishment

We know today that inner strength and motivation can sustain people in times of trouble. Our literature is filled with stories of persons who survived Hitler's concentration camps, the Bataan death march in the Phillipines, crippling accidents, and all sorts of trauma and mayhem. Certain individuals seem to have a spark that keeps them going.

> **Ruby B., female, student, age six. In 1960 her school was being integrated in Louisiana. Each day the federal marshals would escort her to school through crowds of hostile adults who threatened her life, spat on her, and called her vile names. This went on for months,**

THE MIND-BODY-SPIRIT CONNECTION

but she gave no signs of cracking under the emotional battering. A psychiatrist who had been called in to study her couldn't understand what fortified this remarkable little girl until Ruby reported, "I pray for them every day—even though sometimes I don't feel much like praying for them—because they don't know what they're doing!"

Ruby was nourished by deep religious and moral convictions that came from her family's words and examples. Though her parents were poor and had little education, they gave her a Christian home, an atmosphere of humility, and a stoic dignity that sustained her during that troubled year.

Dr. Robert Coles, a psychiatrist who studied Ruby, had this to say about her and others affected by poverty, economic struggle, war, and other strife: "Remember, those who are poor often have no reason to feel self-important. For them humility and humbleness are an everyday fact of life.... And, this, by the way, is what I think Christ had in mind when he lectured to people—and talked about the poor getting into heaven. I think he was talking about those who somehow have learned to feel poor and humble in spirit as against those who feel very smug about themselves."

Each day before Ruby left for school her grandmother would say, "Don't forget to pray for those white folks at the school—even if at times you don't feel like it!" And Ruby prayed and she received spiritual nourishment in the process. The

Holy Spirit strengthened her throughout those troubled times.

I'd like now to share with you some ways I have found that help feed and strengthen my spirit.

Six spiritual strengtheners

1. Pray regularly for yourself and others. The cornerstone of all spiritual nourishment is prayer. Seek the help of the Holy Spirit as counselor. When God responds with advice that seems misdirected, keep in mind what Jesus prayed to his father in the garden of Gethsemane: "Yet not as I will, but as you will" (Matt. 26:39). We were not created to rely completely on our own personal resources. Mother Teresa once said, "The task for recovery is not what *you* want—but what Jesus wants for you!"

2. Fill the cup of good will. Make it a habit to help one or more persons in some way each day. Listen to a troubled friend. Teach a child. Work in a soup kitchen. Visit an aged person. Remember Jesus said that when you give a thirsty person a drink of water, you are giving him a drink. Then *two* cups of good will have been filled! Mother Teresa considers service a privilege, not an obligation. When Malcolm Muggeridge asked her, "What do you say to people who are spiritually hungry?" she replied, "I tell them to go to the poor. There you will find God in solidarity with them."

3. Attend religious services. Keep yourself involved with a church or synagogue or religious group on a regular basis. Enjoy the heritage that is offered by the preaching, the Bible, the people, the artwork, the music, the service of worship, and even the architecture. Let the *past* nourish the present. Gain strength in the process.

4. *Collect people, not things.* Try to establish priorities in a materialistic society. When the choice is there, choose people over things. Nourish friendships and relationships. Be a collector of people. Follow the simple life. "It is more blessed to give than to receive." (Acts 20:35) Enjoy things without owning them. Don't spend so much time and effort in materialistic pursuits.

5. *Accentuate the positive.* Choose causes and people that accentuate the positive and help your community and the world about you. There are so many "downers" and so many negative remarks tossed our way each day that you must consciously spend time *thinking positively*. Think about the *good* things that happen each day to you and others.

6. *Minimize the negative.* Seek constructive ways to deal with negative, hostile people and situations in your life that add little and subtract much from your energy. When confronted with a situation to which you react angrily or negatively, try to think of it in a *positive* way, or at least in a "neutral" way. Remember the words of Paul, "In all things God works for the good of those who love him ..." (Rom. 8:28); "Do not let the sun go down while you are still angry" (Eph. 4:26).

Jesus said this to his disciples and so he says it to us today, "If you love me, you will obey what I command. And I will ask the Father, and he will give you another Counselor to be with you forever—the Spirit of truth. The world cannot accept him, because it neither sees him nor knows him. But you know him for he lives with you and will be in you. I will not leave you as orphans; I will come to you" (John 14:15-18).

I saw a sign recently. It was near a church and had this headline, GLUE FACTORY. Underneath was this message, "Let Christ be the *glue* that helps you and your family stay together."

All the evidence I've been able to read and experience and is presented in this mind-body-spirit chapter, tells me that healthy individuals must have this connection. It is therefore important that we understand and use this glue. Ruby B. used it during her ordeal. Granger Westberg found it makes a difference in who survived surgery. Mother Teresa uses it. You, too, will find that it helps you stay glued together!

CHAPTER SIX

Fitness:
Its Whys and
Hows

I t's been my experience that you don't have to know the whys or hows that make things work in order to use them. The TV set in my study is one example and the computer in the basement is another. There are many examples in the medical world, but three come to mind:

1. Aspirin.   Acetyl salicylic acid has been used in the medical world for over 100 years for its antiarthritic actions. It worked. In proper dosage it was safe and cheap. But it took until the 1980s before scientists finally uncovered the reason why it worked (by blocking conversion of arachidonic· acid to prostaglandins).

2. Chelation therapy.   Treatment with ethylene diamine tetracetic acid (EDTA) has been a safe and effective nonsurgical treatment for cardiovascular disease and other problems for 40 years. Only in 1984, however, has its effect on removing free radicals (see Chapter 2) been able to account for the beneficial results observed in age-associated disorders.

3. Fitness.   Coaches, physicians, and scientists have known for decades that individuals who are physically fit benefit in ways such as better sleep, improved appetite, increased energy and stamina, better digestion, and improved disposition. However, it has only been in recent years that researchers have demonstrated the specific reasons.

This chapter will describe some ways—and the reasons for them—to get you on the best road of fitness for you. Information will be provided on energy expenditures of certain sports and useful guidelines offered on conditioning methods.

Vivian N., 50 years, salesperson. Viv was told by her doctor that her recurring backache would continue unless she got into some regular exercise. But her new direct sales business was going so well and it took so much of her time and energy that she replied, "Doc, just where am I going to find 30 minutes a day to exercise? I'm already booked from 8:00 in the morning until 9:00 at night. There's no way!"

First—the bad news

Despite a remarkable increase in running, jogging, tennis, hiking, biking, and cross-country skiing, most Americans are still not exercising. Despite the explosion of health spas, fitness clubs, and all sorts of new exercise apparatus, the words uttered 35 years ago by the former president of the University of Chicago, Paul Hutchins, reflect the attitude many Americans have today about exercise: "Whenever I get the urge to exercise, I lie down until the urge passes!"

FITNESS: ITS WHYS AND HOWS

A recent study at the University of Minnesota by Robert Jeffery and Aaron Folsom showed that adults who live in the Minneapolis-St. Paul area— a part of the country noted for an interest in sports activities—are getting fatter despite the boom in fitness, low-calorie foods, and weight-loss programs. From 1973-1974 to 1980-1981 the percentage of overweight people rose among men over 40 and among all women.

Here are some observations of researchers who analyzed the results of the study:

- Smoking cessation, most common among middle-aged men in recent years, is usually accompanied by increased body weight.
- The prevalence of overweight in the U.S. population is substantial and may be increasing.
- More men than women—37.5% vs. 30%—said they had reduced successfully.
- Most of the dieters lost weight on their own (only 3.3% of the men and 22.6% of the women enrolled in formal weight-loss programs).
- Of those who enrolled in weight-loss programs, such as Weight Watchers, 29% of the females and 11.5% of the males found the programs were successful.

Another concern is that although the fitness movement has been rolling at high speed for 10 years or more, the experts are still divided about the benefits in longevity and decreased heart disease. Even Kenneth H. Cooper, the physician from Dallas, Texas, who perhaps more than any other single person is credited with getting millions of

Americans out of their chairs and into running shoes, says we have been acting largely on faith. Allan Parachini of the *Los Angeles Times* reports that Cooper and the readers of his several books, "may have taken their original enthusiasm for aerobics a bit too far, a little too soon."

This is the reason that Dr. Cooper has recruited a research staff and organized a massive study of what happens to people who change their habits and embrace aerobics. The study will last for years—probably decades—and already involves more than 20,000 research subjects at the Institute for Aerobic Research.

Part of the study has already been completed and turned up a significant surprise for the scientists. In a questionnaire returned by more than 12,000 Cooper Clinic patients *nearly half* reported they had orthopedic problems. Although not all of the problems were due to sports or running, Cooper's survey suggests there may be a higher incidence of injury to bone structures over those who exercise compared to those who don't. Although the study is not completed, it does represent a concern and shows that much more research is needed to resolve the issue. I find many men, especially those in the "40-plus" age bracket, with knee, elbow, and foot complaints related to their pursuit of fitness.

Dr. Rob Roy McGregor, a podiatrist, marathoner, and running shoe designer from Brookline, Massachusetts, also sees such problems. McGregor indicated these pains of fitness (sportaches) are conditions that have to be handled by the individuals themselves. "A sportache bothers you," he says, "while you're [doing] your favorite sport. . . . The classic example is the runner who goes to the doctor with a pain in his knee. . . . When he's not running, he doesn't have pain. That's a sportache."

Other common examples McGregor described are the tennis player with a sore wrist, the swimmer with shoulder pain, and the golfer with elbow pain. All have a common bond—sharp twinges of pain during exertion. If not handled well they lead to inflammation and full-blown medical problems.

According to McGregor, sportaches are the result of two things: (1) The forces of the sport are too much for the body—the individuals must reduce the intensity of the force in order to continue playing; and (2) limited tolerance is less than it should be because of poor technique or inadequate conditioning.

When these problems begin McGregor says you must become a "fitness detective." He has developed a formula to help in the investigation. It is called EEVeTec (pronounced *evah-tech),* an acronym for the five factors needed to eliminate sportaches: Equipment, Environment, Velocity, Technique, and Conditioning. These are described in the book *EEVeTech* (Houghton Mifflin, 1982).

Here is how McGregor says you should analyze the five factors:

Equipment. Whatever the sport, a few basic equipment adjustments are always possible. A runner with foot, ankle, or knee pain should check out different shoes; someone with tennis elbow could consider changing rackets, etc.

Environment. A change in *where* you conduct your sport or fitness activity may make the difference. For example, thousands of runners could eliminate running related problems by changing their running surface to one that is smoother or has less slope or other characteristics.

Velocity. By reducing the velocity of the moves and the turns at the first sign of pain, trouble can be minimized.

Technique. Proper technique is good preventive medicine. It places key joints of your body as *close* as possible to their most stable position so that they may absorb and transmit peak force loads more efficiently.

Conditioning. Adequate strength and flexibility enable the individual to achieve and hold the stable position. Before engaging in the sport do at least 10 minutes of warm-up calesthenics and slow stretching, and when finished, spend 10 minutes in cool-down activity.

Now—the good news

The good news still predominates the scene. Despite the forces of our sedentary, high-calorie life, there is dramatically increased participation in running, jogging, tennis, biking, and healthsports activities of all kinds. *TIME* magazine estimated that in 1981 a record 70 million Americans—almost half the adult population—practiced "some form of corporeal self-betterment." This figure is up from a report in 1960, when only 24% of people surveyed worked out.

This interest in fitness has been accompanied by a wild shopping spree. The following has been spent on fitness-related equipment and activities:

- $4 billion for health clubs and corporate fitness centers.
- $1 billion in all kinds of sport shoes (with perhaps a third worn for fashion or comfort rather than fitness).
- $1 billion for outdoor bicycles and gear.
- $1 billion for swimming pools, goggles, fins, etc.
- $400 million in stationary bikes.
- $240 million for barbells and aerobic dance programs.

At the same time the numbers of participants have greatly increased. It is estimated there are now:

- 30 million confirmed runners in the United States.
- 27 million tennis players, bikers, hikers, swimmers, and others.
- 13 million weight lifters and biceps builders.

The fashion designers and athletic outfitters of the women's world have responded to the fitness boom with jazzercise tights and leotards, running outfits for summer and winter, and sports attire for 15 million female runners in America. Magazines are full of fashion pictures showing Farrah

Fawcett, Jaclyn Smith, and other celebrities using their latest togs.

The ultimate fitness experience, super-spas, are described by one skeptic as "now able to reduce your *weight*, *worries* and *wallet* all at the same time."

The "Sehnert Do-It-Yourself Plan"

Like most of the over 100 million American men or women who should begin an exercise plan— but whose budgets won't permit them the luxury of a trip to one of the super spas—you can settle for the Sehnert Do-It-Yourself Plan. But before launching into an exercise program, it's important to consider questions like these: Who shouldn't exercise at all? When is exercise risky? How should I start? How do I gear up?

Who shouldn't exercise at all?

The American Medical Association's Committee on Exercise and Physical Fitness has said that 5% to 10% of the population have such significant medical problems that they shouldn't exercise at all. They are individuals with these conditions:

- Active or recent myocarditis (inflammation of the heart muscle)
- Congestive heart failure
- Arrythmia from third degree A-V heart block or if using a fixed rate pacemaker
- Ventricular aneurysm (ballooning of the heart wall)

- Aortic aneurysm (ballooning of parts of the major heart vessel that runs from the heart through the chest and abdomen)
- Congenital heart disease with cyanosis (bluish skin color)
- Recent pulmonary embolism (blood clot in the lung)
- Liver degeneration (liver failure).

Who should be careful about exercise?

The same A.M.A. committee has recommended that people who have certain medical problems *should check with a physician* because exercise is risky. Here is a list of those conditions:

- Acute or chronic infectious disease
- Diabetes that is not well controlled
- Marked obesity
- Psychosis or severe neurosis
- Central nervous system disease
- Musculo-skeletal disease involving spine and lower extremities
- Active liver disease
- Renal disease with nitrogen retention (kidney failure)
- Severe anemia (iron deficiency in the blood)
- Significant hypertension (diastolic high blood pressure)
- Angina pectoris or other signs of myocardial insufficiency (chest pain on exertion)
- Cardiomegaly (malformation of the heart)

- Arrythmia from second degree A-V block, ventricular tachycardia or atrial fibrillation (irregular or abnormal fast heartbeats)
- Significant disease of heart valves or larger blood vessels
- Congenital heart disease without cyanosis (bluishness)
- Phlebothrombosis or thrombophlebitis (inflammation of veins)
- Current use of drugs such as reserpine, propranolol hydrochloride, guanethidine sulfate, guinidine sulfate, nitroglycerin (or other vascular dilators), procainamide hydrocholoride, digitalis, catecholamines, ganglionic blocking agents, insulin, or psychotropic drugs.

How should I start?

Now, if you have excluded yourself from those two categories, you are ready to start with a preconditioning program for about one month. Start slowly and remember that your joints, bones, and muscles need some start-up time. Here is a way to begin:

1. Get up a half hour early and take a brisk walk, jog, or bike for 15 minutes before breakfast.
2. Use your feet and rest your car. When you must drive to work or to the grocery store, park in the farthest corner of the lot; then walk to and from your car.
3. On the way to work, get off the bus or the train several blocks early and walk the rest of the way. At work, use the stairs instead of elevators.
4. At noon, "brown-bag it" and engage in some sort of exercise program for half hour with the time saved.

5. Take "exercise breaks" instead of "coffee breaks," walking briskly up and down the halls or stairs.
6. After work, instead of the two martinis before dinner, take two laps around the block.

Now, it's time to select a sport or activity that you will enjoy on a regular basis—preferably three times a week. You may choose from individual or group activities as shown in the following table.

Sports and Activities that Promote Fitness

Individual Activities	Group Activities
Bicycling	Badminton
Calisthenics	Basketball
Chopping wood	Canoeing
Hiking	Dancing
Horseback riding	Fencing
Jogging	Golf (no carts allowed)
Jumping	Handball
Rowing	Jazzercise
Running	Judo
Skating	Karate
Skiing (cross-country)	Ping-pong
Skiing (downhill)	Racquetball
Swimming	Soccer
Walking (briskly)	Squash
	Tennis
	Water-skiing
	Wrestling

Activities you choose are best if they give you an opportunity to:

- *Move.* The benefit from walking, biking, hiking, or jogging is that these activities burn up calories.
- *Stretch and breathe deeply.* Deep breathing and stretching help you to relieve tension and to relax. These movements should be a part of any exercise you choose.
- *Bend, twist, and swing.* Flexibility and agility are as important as muscular endurance and strength. Remember that flexibility refers to the range of movements of the joints.
- *Enjoy yourself.* When exercise is enjoyable, it's relaxing and gives physical, mental, and social benefits.
- *Set your own pace.* Take three or four months of training to achieve your target pulse.
- *Do aerobic activity.* This type of exercise should be intense enough to increase your heart rate, make you perspire and breathe so rapidly that you puff when you talk. After warming up, activity should be sustained for 15 minutes to provide aerobic conditioning effects.

Here are the energy expenditures for some common activities:

Activity	Calories Burned per Hour
Bicycling (5.5 m.p.h.)	210
Gardening	240
Golfing	250
Bowling	270
Playing tennis (doubles)	350
Walking (3.5 m.p.h.)	350

Playing ping-pong	350
Chopping wood	400
Playing tennis (singles)	450
Downhill skiing	450
Playing handball	550
Doing vigorous calisthenics	550
Dancing (fast)	600
Bicycling (13 m.p.h.)	660
Swimming	750
Running (10 m.p.h.)	900
Cross-country skiing	1000

How do I gear up?

Once you have started the program and are starting to firm up the flabby muscles, during the next two months these are four simple rules to follow:

1. Take the talk test. You should be able to talk in a normal way while you exercise. If you can't, you're working too hard—or running too fast—and should slow down.

2. Warm up and cool down. Always do stretching and warm-up exercises before starting your activity. Do knee lifts, back stretches, knee bends, and trunk twists as shown on page 90 before you start. When you are ready to run, begin with a slow trot. Finish with a cool-down walk.

3. Don't be intimidated. Do your own thing, at your own speed, in your own way.

4. Learn your body's capabilities. If you are tight-jointed and stiff, you may need stretching

SELFCARE/WELLCARE

or limbering calisthenics for several weeks before
starting an exercise program.

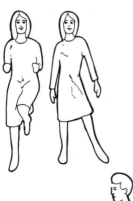

1. Knee-lifts
Begin by gentle bending
of one knee. Then lift up
knee and stretch foot out
to side. Do four knee lifts
with one leg, then switch
to four counts other leg.
Complete four to six
pairs of lifts.

2. Pedaling
Begin by gentle pedaling
action, rolling up from
heel to toe, alternating
feet. Body is entirely relaxed. Build up to gentle
jogging on the spot, lifting feet slightly off the
ground, and continue
for half a minute.

3. Knee Bends and Arm Swings
Put your feet apart; do a
gentle knee bend and
straighten up. Keep up a
fast rhythm. Then add
arm swings, any way,
and continue for 20 to 30
seconds.

FITNESS: ITS WHYS AND HOWS

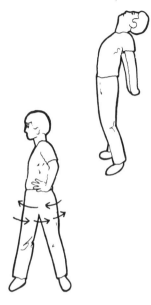

4. **Back Exercise**
   Bend knees slightly; clasp hands behind back. Slowly pull shoulders and head back; arch upper back, keeping elbows straight. Hold; relax head and back, drooping shoulders forward. Repeat six to eight times.

5. **Trunk twists**
   Set feet apart, knees slightly bent, hands on hips. Twist to one side, gently, three times and face center on fourth count. Repeat to opposite side. Complete six to eight pairs of twists.

Exercises such as cross-country skiing, running, swimming, and bicycling not only burn up the most calories but offer aerobic benefits to your heart if you do them for 15-20 minutes. You can see if you are achieving this by calculating your target pulse. Take your pulse either on the wrist or near the base of your thumb or on your neck at the angle of your jaw. Count the pulse for 15 seconds and multiply by four. Then follow these guidelines to calculate your target pulse:

- If you are in poor condition, subtract your age from 150. This is your maximum (or target) pulse while exercising.

• If you are in fair to good condition, subtract your
age from 170. This is your maximum (or target)
pulse while exercising.

In addition to aerobic exercises, there are anaerobic, isotonic, and isometric exercises. Here's
a review of what these terms mean:

Aerobic. Exercise that can be carried on for
15 or more minutes is generally aerobic. Aerobic
exercise is steady, "nonstop" activity. Examples
include swimming, jogging, cycling, and walking.

Anaerobic. Exercise that is short in duration,
"stop-and-go" in rhythm, and low intensity in effort. Examples include tennis and golf.

Isotonic. Rhythmic, repetitive exercise that
involves motion. Improved blood circulation
comes from the alternation between tensing and
relaxing the muscles. Isotonic exercises can be
either aerobic (calisthenics, horseshoe pitching,
archery) or anaerobic (weight lifting).

Isometric. Exercise with very little movement, like pushing your hands against each other
or lifting or pushing against an object that won't
move. Although isometric exercises may develop
muscle tone and can make you stronger, they don't
improve your heart conditioning and may even be
dangerous for heart patients. That is because they
can cause the muscles involved to get shorter and
tense up, squeezing blood vessels and decreasing
the flow of blood through the heart.

By the time you have spent three months in the
Sehnert Do-It-Yourself Plan your muscles will be
firmer and you will feel better, look better, and

experience more stamina. Your emotions will be more tranquil because exercise washes away the endorphans (a brain chemical that can accumulate and cause depression). You will feel better even when you don't reach aerobic levels of exertion. Exercise has been called "the safest tranquilizer," but it's much more important than that—it's absolutely essential for high-level wellness.

Remember this axiom as you develop your plan: We used to stay fit in our struggle to *survive.* Now, in order to survive, we must struggle to stay *fit.*

CHAPTER SEVEN

How to Beat the High Costs of Medical Care

> **Only Cure for Medical System is to Put Lid on Costs** —*The Washington Post*
>
> **Health Care Soon Up to \$1 Billion a Day** —*American Medical News*
>
> **Health-Care Spending Hits Record Share of GNP** —*New York Times*
>
> **Soaring Costs: U.S. Health Bill Jumps 15.1%** —*Time*
>
> **Health Care Expenditures: The Approaching Crisis** —*Mayo Clinic Proceedings*

These headlines tell a familiar story about the economics of medical care. John H. Herrell of the Mayo Clinic's Section of Financial Analysis and Planning, in an article that accompanied the last headline, said, "To understand this crisis, one must first compare present utilization with past utilization, and present health care and medical care expenditures with other expenditures. The sobering conclusion one reaches when analyzing the past medical care expenditures in light of future demographics is that, unless something radically changes, the percentage of the gross national product (GNP) devoted to medical care in the year 2010 will be dramatically different than it is today" (J.H. Herrel, "Health Care Expenditures: The Approaching Crisis," *Mayo Clinic Proceedings* [1980] 55:708-710).

The stories that accompanied the other headlines described a variety of solutions—some simple and some complex. They offered many opinions about the "culprits" behind the high costs: the doctors, health insurance managers, hospital administrators, politicians, union leaders, and last, but not least, the patients and their families.

Like other complex issues our nation faces today—inflation, environmental pollution, poverty, social justice, women's and minority's rights, quality education—there are few simple answers. For every hospital service or test there is a cost. For every insurance benefit there is a premium. For every environmental safeguard there is an increase in the cost of the product to the consumer. For every improvement in social justice or legal right there is a salary for enforcement. For quality there is an increase in taxes. There are no free lunches.

Who are the bad guys?

In order to understand the dilemma of high cost medical care, let's first take a look at the economic dynamics behind the headlines. The facts show that total annual expenditures in the United States for medical care and other forms of health-related activities increased 1500% between 1950 and 1978.

Who are the "bad guys" in this drama? It's not so simple.

Doctors. The person who reads that most doctors earn about $100,000 per year believes this increase in health-related expenditures is going into the doctor's pockets. But economist Herrell points out, "Although physician's fees have risen faster than the consumer price index, they have risen only slightly faster than fees for service industries as a whole over the past 22 years."

He also points out that if you cut the doctor's net income in half you would only reduce the total cost of health care "by approximately 5% one time."

To help understand medical economics, it is important to understand how today's pricing practices got started. In the 1950s, doctors found that although patients resented paying more than $3-$5 for the doctor's visit ($3 was the average office visit fee that was charged when I started practicing medicine in 1954 in York, Nebraska), they didn't object to large markups on simple laboratory procedures and such things as X-ray examinations.

From this emerged a fee structure in which physicians billed their time as a "loss leader" and made their income from procedures. Over the years since, this produced two types of medical incomes and practices: *procedure-oriented* specialists such as surgeons, pathologists, and radiologists, and *exam-oriented* doctors such as family doctors, pediatricians, and internists. The procedure-oriented physicians came out the big winners in this two-tiered economic arrangement because of "usual and customary" fees set by insurance companies and governmental agencies. The more tests done, the higher the medical income. The principle driving this has been the false assumption that "more is better." This has been fueled by an explosive growth in medical technology plus the technicians needed to run the machines and interpret the results obtained.

Health-insurance managers. Because of unbending adherence to the "usual and customary" fees and procedures and emphasis on lab tests, companies have inadvertantly increased the cost of medical care. Managers gladly accept lower procedure fees but refuse to allow a portion of the savings to be transferred to examination fees, education, and counseling time. This makes it easier—and more profitable—for doctors to send patients to the lab than talk to them. The result is that patients often complain, "The doctors never talk to me!" This is ironic in view of the sage advice once given to me in medical school, allegedly from the famous medical professor, Sir William Osler: "Doctors, if you will only listen to the patients, they will *tell you what's wrong with them!*"

Hospital administrators. Anyone who has studied the explosive growth of health-care costs will tell you that the greatest costs today are in the hospital sector. When I graduated from medical school in 1953, nearly all the hospitals, except the university hospitals, were run by nurses or religious personnel. Hospitals were truly nonprofit and run as community resources, with large volunteer staffs and free service from nursing students. When I graduated I went to Henry Ford Hospital because they paid "high" intern salaries of $150 per month at a time when most hospitals paid nothing but room, board, and uniforms!

Then the Golden Age of Medicine dawned, and a new breed of hospital administrators moved in. They were smart, well-trained, and knew how to build surgical wings, add maternity services, acquire fancy laboratory X-ray and computer systems—and *make money!* This expansion was fueled by Hill-Burton, Medicare, and Medicaid and the liberal health-insurance benefits received by more and more employees. (The strength of the HMO movement in America in the 1970s and 1980s was in lowering costs by keeping patients *out* of these expensive hospitals.)

From 1960 to 1980 pay scales for nurses and staff skyrocketed. The sophisticated equipment and skilled persons to run them such as the nurses, physical therapists, radiology and laboratory technologists—all with credentials and licensure (to restrict entry of the less trained)—led to the demise of the minimum-wage hospital worker of the 1940s and '50s. The house staff physicians at the Mayo Clinic, for instance, got salary increases of 944% (compared to an increase of 207% in the consumer price index) between 1950 and 1979.

Another cost that soared sky high was that of professional liability, the cost of insurance to protect the hospital managers and staff from malpractice claims. Again, in a report from one of the Mayo-affiliated hospitals, the premiums jumped

HOW TO BEAT THE HIGH COSTS OF MEDICAL CARE

from $42,000 annually to $200,000 for *less cover-age*, despite the fact it employed no physicians and had never paid a claim in excess of $40,000.

Politicians. The congressmen and senators in Washington completely altered the economics of medicine with Medicare and Medicaid. This legislation stimulated demand for services at an annual growth rate of 16.5%. Although implemented in 1966 to help low-income elders, Medicare *now pays a lower portion of the medical and hospital bills* than when it was started.

The Hill-Burton Act was passed by Congress to increase the number of hospital facilities around the country. It was so successful that it provided an oversupply of facilities, so that most hospitals now have only 50%-70% occupancy. (Competitive factors are forcing smaller hospitals to merge with others or close in many communities.) The Act also made the provision that free care must be offered if a family earns less than $17,800 (the poverty level for a family of six). The cost for staffing empty beds, services to over-65 patients, and free care to low-income families is then passed on to the "paying customers."

Union leaders. During World War II, when prices and wages were frozen by orders from President Roosevelt, one of the benefits in the package negotiated by many union leaders was the agreement by the employer to pay health insurance premiums for hospital and medical care. Although wages were frozen, union members—and eventually everyone else—got more take-home pay because they didn't have to pay for their own insurance coverage. The amount of this fringe benefit grew over the years because through legislation and tax changes employers could provide unlimited quantities of benefits on a *tax-free basis.* Employees liked it because with tax brackets rising from inflation, these benefits soon became more valuable than wages. Union leaders liked it because they could go to the bargaining table and come away with employers providing first half, then two-thirds, and eventually all of "first dollar coverage" (no deductibles, no copayments, but the entire cost of health-care coverage).

Government bureaucrats. Another hidden but major cost for health care both in the hospital and medical office is that of administrative "red tape" and regulation. This comes from programs such as Occupational Safety and Health Administration (OSHA), Worker's Compensation, Professional Standards Review Organization (PSRO), Medical Care Evaluation (MCE), and a whole bevy of public health and public assistance programs. Many of these were added by congressional mandates beginning in the Great Society years of President Johnson and were then promulgated by succeeding layers of regulatory edicts and decisions. All were started by well-meaning attempts to solve a problem. Each probably created more problems than it solved and added to the high costs of getting sick or injured.

Patients and their families. When you or a member of your family gets sick or injured, rational thought about medical economics may go out the window. Recently as I walked through the emergency room area of a hospital, I noticed a distraught man standing beside a woman who was sitting in a wheelchair. As I walked by I heard him say, "Do it the best way you can. *Nothing is too good for my wife!*"

We have arrived at a situation in our society in which we have had an explosive growth of medical services fueled by government funds, dramatized by television and movies, and financed by employers. This has resulted in an increased *quantity* of care per patient, with the unproved assumption that this represents increased *quality*. Unfortunately, the cost/benefit trade-offs have rarely, if ever, been made. The assumption that "more is better" cannot be claimed. In fact, "less is better" may be a safer, certainly less expensive, goal for us, our families, and our society.

On becoming a wiser buyer/user

A doctor friend of mine once said, "In America decisions are made by voting with your feet or your dollar." By that he meant that if you don't like a service or product, you go elsewhere and find a better or cheaper product or service.

This can happen in any free and open marketplace, and I see it happening in today's medical marketplace. That is the reason that my program at Georgetown University, the "Course for Activated Patients," caught the attention of the media.

It is also why employers like the idea. The program follows these simple guidelines:

- *At home*—record your illness or injury symptoms and use a selfcare book to help handle common problems.
- *In the doctor's office*—ask questions about your diagnosis and get involved in your treatment decisions.
- *If hospitalized*—keep track of the services you receive.

There is a great interest in home health care and the concept of medical selfcare. A rapidly increasing number of Americans are interested in options other than today's high-tech, complex, and expensive medical care.

One astute observer to today's health care system said, "It's like a giant Calder mobile—you move one of the panels and all the rest start moving." I like that analogy, because when a patient enters the doctor's office or the emergency room at the hospital or submits an insurance claim, the parts start moving—and the cash registers start ringing.

Individuals can make a difference by the choices they make as buyers and users of health-care services and products. An increasing number of businesses and organizations recognize this and have started health promotion and wellness programs on the assumption that the best way to contain costs is to keep employees from *entering the system in the first place* by helping them stay well.

However, the reality is that persons do get sick and injured and are involved in life events that require professional help, and individuals have family members and friends who have health problems and need assistance. Because of this, we do need to become wiser buyers/users of health-care resources. We do at times need to become Activated Patients and need guidelines.

For such situations, I have the following list of dos and don'ts:

Guidelines of Things You Can Do (to Become a Wiser Buyer/User)

1. **Join the People's Medical Society.**   The benefits include a newsletter, plus books and materials for use by you or your family. The address for this organization is: 14 East Minor St., Emmaus PA 18049.

2. **Subscribe to *Medical Self-Care* magazine.** Subscriptions for *Medical Self-Care* may be obtained by writing to: P.O. Box 1000, Pt. Reyes CA 94956.

3. **Establish a home health reference library.**   A good bibliography is available from: Planetree Health Resource Center, 2040 Webster St., San Francisco CA 94115.

4. **Take medical selfcare classes.**   A listing of contact persons around the country who are involved in classes is available from *Medical Self-Care* (see above).

5. **Equip yourself with some medical equipment.**   Medical equipment such as blood pressure kits and examination tools are available from a variety of places. The "Family Black Bag" can

be bought from: Marshall Electronics, 600 Barclay Blvd., Lincolnshire IL 60069. A whole series of equipment including the Earscope can be obtained from Self-Care Catalog, P.O. Box 1000, Pt. Reyes CA 94956. A number of "checkup kits" are now available from: Boditestor, Inc., P.O. Box 10666, Marina Del Rey CA 90291.

6. **Establish a health partnership with a physician.** An increasing number of physicians, especially family doctors and pediatricians, have education classes as integral parts of their medical practice. If you have a doctor who prefers a more authoritarian, no-questions-asked type of practice, and is uncomfortable in such a health partnership, then it would be a good idea to shop around for a new doctor. Some specific details are found in Chapter 11 of my recently revised book, *How To Be Your Own Doctor, Sometimes* (New York: Grosset and Dunlap, 1975, 1985).

7. **Use the Ask-the-Doctor Checklist when you go to the physician.** See p. 109 for a copy of this checklist.

8. **Don't go to the doctor alone.** Lowell S. Levin, professor in the Yale University Department of Epidemiology and Public Health, has the following to say about taking someone with you when going to the doctor:*

   ● The doctor senses the presence of an observer in the room and may feel more inclined to be communicative and supportive.

   ● Your companion also can help both you and

---

*Reprinted from "People's Medical Society Newsletter."

the doctor by bringing up questions and concerns you may have had before entering the doctor's examining room.

● Facts important to your doctor's diagnosis and treatment plan also can be raised by the friend or relative. These could include, for example, factors concerning your lifestyle or work environment that escaped your own notice simply because they are so commonplace in your life.

● It is really helpful to have someone who can remind the doctor about practical things he or she should consider in deciding about care after surgery, such as who will feed the children or the fact that you may live in a fourth-floor walk-up and won't be able to negotiate stairs.

● Your chances of remembering what was said by your doctor are at least doubled by having a friend who was there. In fact, you are generally in a better position to objectively evaluate the whole experience and to make further decisions about your care. You aren't alone.

9. **Don't be afraid to say no or ask why.**   In this day of informed consent and with a Patient's Bill of Rights in the laws of many states to protect the patients' right to know, the two words *no* and *why* are safeguards. (Many insurance companies pay for second surgical opinions, which can offer another physician's viewpoint about proposed surgery.) You also have the right to ask why an X-ray or test is being ordered and what it will cost. Patients and their families have the option to say no to surgical or medical treatments.

10. **When a prescription is to be written, ask the doctor and pharmacist about generic drugs.**

Most people are aware of the fact that generic drugs cost from 30% to 50% less than trade or brand-name drugs. Ask your pharmacist or doctor to provide this option for you. The drug will save money, and the generic form is almost always equally effective.

A national plan for lowering health-care costs

Now with those guidelines for your personal actions, I would also like to recommend some things that *others* (business executives, politicians, and planners) can do to help lower health-care costs.

Guidelines of Things Others Can Do to Lower Health Care Costs

1. **Avoid "first dollar" coverage in health insurance policies.** "First dollar" coverage describes health insurance policies in which the subscriber receives 100% coverage of doctor and hospital bills. Other policies have $100, $250, and $1000 "deductibles," which mean that the user pays the out-of-pocket portion of the bill, and when the deductible has been exceeded, the insurance company pays the rest. Example: an individual policy from one company, for which I paid $916 per year, was replaced by a policy from another company (with $500 deductible) that costs only $481 per year. The coverage was otherwise identical.

2. **Encourage competition to increase efficiency of health-care systems.** Competition benefits

HOW TO BEAT THE HIGH COSTS OF MEDICAL CARE

the consumer. In the Minneapolis-St. Paul area, for example, over 40% of the population uses health maintenance organizations (HMOs) and such firms. Fee-for-service practitioners, preferred provider organizations (PPOs), hospitals, and various other provider groups are all competing against each other. It has helped improve the quality of medical services and contain costs.

3. **Impose a "means test" for Medicare recipients who have private financial resources.** Richard Corlin, M.D., of Santa Monica, California, vice-chairman of the American Medical Association Council on Long-Range Planning and Development, proposed, "...'a reasonable high means test should be applied to government funded programs such as Medicare" (*American Medical News*, May 11, 1984).

4. **Increase taxes on tobacco and alcohol.** Because abuses of these products account for at least 25% of medical costs, high taxes on tobacco and alcohol have been found to be successful in the Scandinavian countries. In Denmark, for instance, a bottle of Scotch whiskey that would cost $10 in the United States costs $40. The same is true of cigarettes, which cost $4 per package in Copenhagen compared to $1 here. These public health measures produced significant decreases in cirrhosis of the liver, lung cancer, and a host of other ills and accidents.

5. **Ask your company to start health promotion/wellness programs.**

6. **Encourage your company to increase cost-consciousness about health benefits and health insurance.**

7. **Ask your company to get health insurance that provides "cafeteria" or "flexible benefits" programs for education options under your health insurance.** American business firms have taken the lead from the National Chamber Foundation (U.S. Chamber of Commerce, 1615 H. St., NW, Washington DC 20062), Health Insurance Association of America (Health Insurance Institute, 1850 K St., NW, Washington DC 20006) and other organizations that provide materials and assistance in starting the programs listed in guidelines 5, 6, and 7.

8. **Ask your company to get health insurance that gives discounts to nonsmokers, runners, and low-risk employees.** There are some insurance companies that already specialize in offering cheaper premiums for low-risk individuals. In the future there will be other companies created to sell such coverage plus offer education and other incentives to keep people healthy.

9. **Encourage your state and federal representatives to revamp or even consider abolishing medical licensing boards.** Lori B. Andrews, a lawyer who works for the American Bar Association and is a lecturer in health and hospital law at the University of Chicago Graduate School of Business, has prepared a major study, *Deregulating Doctoring: Do Medical Licensure Laws Meet Today's Health Care Needs?* Andrews points out that as the American public has become more interested in prevention, selfcare, and the use of nonphysician practitioners—for either philosophical or cost reasons— it is not only unfair but also inefficient and perhaps even dangerous for the medical establishment to run the show under the broad protection of state

medical practice acts. Andrews' book is available from the People's Medical Society.

With a better understanding of the health-care system and the way it interacts and with some practical guidelines for action, you can become a wiser buyer/ user in today's medical marketplace.

Ask-the-Doctor-Checklist

Before the visit (Complete this part yourself)

1. Why am I going to the doctor?

   (List the main reason) _____

   _____

2. The symptoms that bother me most:
   (Use the SOAP System in Chapter 10 to describe)

   _____

   _____

   _____

3. The observations I have made:
   (Using SOAP System in Chapter 10 to measure)

   _____

   _____

   _____

4. What medicines or "pills" am I taking regularly now?

   (Please list) _____

   _____

SELFCARE/WELLCARE

During the visit (Complete with help of doctor)

1. What is wrong with me? _____

_____

2. Why did I get it and how can I prevent it next time?

_____

_____

3. Is it catching or will it spread?

    No ____Yes (describe protective measures) _____

_____

4. Are there any lab reports or diagnostic findings I should know about?

    No ____Yes (list) _____

_____

5. Is there any medicine?

    No ____Yes (list) _____

6. (If yes, is it available in a less expensive "generic"

    form?) _____

7. Are there special instructions, concerns, or side effects I should understand about the medicine?

    No ____Yes (describe) _____

_____

After the visit (Complete with help of doctor or office aide)

1. Am I to return for another visit?

    No ____Yes (when) _____

HOW TO BEAT THE HIGH COSTS OF MEDICAL CARE

2. What should I do at home?

    a) Diet_____

    b) Activity _____

    c) Treatments _____

    d) Precautions _____

3. Am I to phone in for lab reports?

    No ____Yes (when) _____

    _____

4. Should I report back to the doctor for any reason?

    No ____Yes (reason) _____

    _____

Alternative Therapies: People in Different Hats

One day I was taking a walk with Maxwell, our family poodle. He was having his usual good time of running and looking and sniffing every tree and shrub. All of a sudden Maxwell froze in his tracks. His back and tail fur bristled. He began to bark—as loud as I had ever heard him—at three teenage boys who came down the steps of our neighbor's house. Apparently what triggered the response was the large floppy hat adorned with feathers and several colored ribbons worn at a rakish angle by one of the boys. My normally friendly dog would have attacked the young man had I not restrained Max with his leash. He didn't stop barking until the boys went into a nearby house and closed the door.

As we continued our stroll, I thought, "You know, we humans also tend to bark at people in different hats. Many of us get upset because people around us have different skin colors, different languages, and different clothes. Such differences are probably behind much of the bigotry, biases, and behaviors that have caused so much trouble for us. It has even led to riots and wars."

It's easy to be suspicious—or even alarmed—about persons who look, talk, act, or even walk in different ways. In the health field, state medical practice boards and the medical establishment often "bark" at professionals in alternative or "nontraditional" therapies, such as chiropractors, faith healers, or acupuncturists. Is this to protect the public or the doctors' own vested interests? Should you seek alternative therapy? Are you likely to be helped or "ripped off"? I'll try to answer these and related questions and concerns in this chapter.

Health workers in different hats

In the fields of health and medicine in the United States, the people in the "different hats" are those who *do not* practice *allopathic* medicine. The term *allopathy* is "the method of treating disease by the use of agents, producing effects different from those of the disease treated." *Homeopathy,* on the other hand, is defined as "a method of treating disease by drugs, given in minute doses, which would produce in a healthy person symptoms similar to those of the disease."

Over the years I have sought out people with different hats. I've learned a lot *about* them, and, more importantly, a lot *from* them. In the process of talking with osteopaths, homeopaths, chiropractors, acupuncturists, faith healers, and others involved in what orthodox physicians call "alternative practices," I have learned that traditional medicine doesn't have all the answers. I've also learned that the vast majority of the alternative practitioners I have met are highly motivated and caring people who are trying their best to help others. I found no evidence that they were hurting their clients or patients.

Now by that, I don't mean to give a sweeping endorsement of *all* alternatives. My intent is merely to state that in my experience, unlike the medical establishment which views alternative practitioners with an often arrogant, hostile attitude, many alternative modalities are worth exploration. There are quacks both inside and outside the A.M.A.

We have all read stories about diabetics who quit taking their insulin because a faith healer told them God had healed them of their affliction. We know of parents who belonged to religious cults and refused medical care for their child because of their beliefs and the child died. We've seen TV stories of psychic surgeons in the Philippines who cured patients of their cancer with their "treatments."

How then does a lay person make wise decisions about the many alternatives? To begin with, let's examine what is presently available in medical care. Today's medical scene can be pictured as a spectrum of traditional and nontraditional practices. (See table on p. 115)

Based on my observations, I estimate that the number of people in the healing arts ("health workers," as my friend, Tom Ferguson, M.D., editor

Spectrum of the Healing Arts in the U.S.

NONTRADITIONAL ⟷ TRADITIONAL
(ALTERNATIVE PRACTICES)   (ORTHODOX PRACTICES)

Unlicensed   Unlicensed | Licensed   Licensed
"New Age"   Cross- | Paramedical   Medical
    Cultural |

    | Licensed   Licensed
    | Nonmedical   "Maverick"
    | Medicine

Licensed Medical:
Primary care physicians
Secondary care
    specialists
Tertiary care specialists

Licensed Paramedical:
Nurses (RN & LPN)
Nurse midwives
Physical therapists
Laboratory & specialty
    technicians
Physician's assistants
Psychologists
Psychiatric social
    workers

**Licensed "Maverick"
    Medicine:**
Holistic practitioners
Healthsports/wellness
    specialists
Orthomolecular medicine
Chelation therapists
Clinical ecologists

Licensed Nonmedical:
Osteopaths
Homeopaths
Chiropractors
Naturopaths
Therapeutic nutritionists

**Unlicensed Cross-
    Cultural:**
Acupuncturists
Yoga teachers
Reiki practitioners
Shiatsu practitioners
TM practitioners
Faith healers

Unlicensed "New Age":
Reflexology
Kinesiology
Iridology
Rolfing
Macrobiotics

of *Medical Self-Care,* calls them), on the left of the line has doubled or tripled since I first began my studies in 1975. Some observers say that the total number of nontraditional healers *will equal the licensed practitioners in the United States by the turn of the century.* Let's look more closely at some of these "alternative practitioners."

Osteopathy. The founder of osteopathy was a physician from Missouri, Dr. Andrew Taylor Still (1828-1917). He developed a complete system of healing by manipulation and bone setting. His basic theory was that structure and function of the human body are interdependent and if the structure of the body becomes altered or abnormal, then the function is altered and illness results. Dr. Still taught "the rule of the artery is supreme," meaning that where arterial blood supply was normal the bodily *structure* would function normally. Abnormality could occur in the spinal column, he believed, and alter blood flow.

Although Dr. Still and his successors developed a system of manipulation, they did not ignore other factors such as dietary deficiencies, the need for muscle strength and physical therapy, and other natural modalities such as good posture and proper breathing.

The traditional American Medical Association's view that osteopathy was cultist and unscientific was dropped in 1961 when the American Osteopathic Association accepted the A.M.A. offer of consolidation and absorption. In 1962 the state of California gave 2200 D.O.s (Doctors of Osteopathy) the option to buy a paper M.D. degree for $65, and 2000 accepted the offer. At the same time the osteopathic college in Los Angeles became an M.D. institution.

There are now 15 D.O. colleges, including state-supported colleges in Oklahoma, Texas, Ohio, West Virginia, New Jersey, and Michigan. Their graduates tend to become small-town general practitioners and provide manipulation and a variety of other medical services. In Great Britain and most European nations, osteopathic-type manipulation is provided by orthopedic surgeons and physical medicine and rehabilitation specialists who assist in recovery of people who have had accidents, strokes, and other injuries.

Homeopathy. Homeopathy is a 200-year-old healing art that is attracting a good deal of consumer interest despite its rejection by mainstream medicine. It was discovered in Germany by S. H. Hahnemann (1755-1843), who formulated the principle, *similia, similibus curatus*—"like is healed by like." He viewed symptoms as expressions of the body's curative processes.

The allopathic physician treats with opposites—decongestants for nasal congestion—and generally believes that "more is better," while homeopaths treat with similars and believe that "less is better." Their remedies are highly diluted and given in the smallest doses possible with the assumption that such small doses stimulate the body's "vital energy" and catalyze the cure. For example, belladonna is a remedy for abdominal pain and is a natural source antispasmodic given in a dose of 1 grain tablet (this is one-fifth the size of an aspirin tablet) every 2 to 4 hours. There are currently about 2000 remedies in the *Homeopathic Pharmacopoeia.*

Penny Righthand, R.N., said in a recent article, "The American Institute of Homeopathy was established in 1844, two years before the founding of the American Medical Association. The A.M.A. refused homeopaths admission in their fledgling society, despite the fact that most of them had been trained in the allopathic medicine of the day. The A.M.A. also expelled some of its members for consulting with homeopaths *(Medical Self-Care,* Winter 1983, p. 36).

In 1911 the Flexner Report rated homeopathy training programs so poorly that foundation and government support was withdrawn and homeopathy almost disappeared from the American medical scene. In England and other countries, however, homeopathy continued to be popular and widely respected. Even today the British Royal Family's physician is a homeopath. The famous Mahatma Gandhi used homeopathic remedies all his life.

Chiropractic. Chiropractic is the largest of the nondrug healing professions. Its practitioners are found in all of the nations of western Europe, Canada, Australia, and New Zealand. Many chiropractic patients feel they can enter into more egalitarian practitioner-patient relationships with their chiropractors than they can with most medical doctors. Through effective political action, doctors of chiropractic (D.C.) have become licensed in all states, and their professional services are included in many insurance plans.

David Palmer founded modern-day chiropractic in 1885 in Davenport, Iowa. There are now 16 schools of chiropractic in the United States. There is a close similarity in the types of problems handled by osteopaths and chiropractors because both are concerned with the functional integrity of the muscular skeletal system, although chiropractors prefer the term "adjustment" to "manipulation." In addition to manual methods, chiropractors use exercise, advice, nutritional guidance, and shoe, seat, bed, and work-position changes.

Acupuncture.   During the last 10 years, according to Michael J. Skolar in *Medical World News* (May 14, 1984), the medical establishment's doubt and hostility toward acupuncture, "... have yielded to an acknowledgment (if sometimes reluctant) that acupuncture (and acupressure) does offer effective treatment for some patients and some disorders.

"In 1974 an expert commission headed by Dr. Jackson W. Riddle—now a member of the A.M.A.'s council for medical affairs—found acupuncture safe and effective. Yet the FDA still considers it investigational, the A.M.A. maintains that it's unproven and many doctors view it as a placebo."

An estimated 2000 physicians in the United States now use acupuncture in pain centers and private offices. Even though this Chinese needling art has been practiced for 4500 years, in the United States it still is in limbo medically and legally. New techniques for sterilization of steel needles and the addition of low frequency current to provide continuous stimulation have improved results. The needles seldom cause bleeding. The typical treatment requires two to eight needles and lasts half an hour. Practitioners insert needles in several of the 367 acupuncture points along 12 meridians or channels to depths of 0.5 to 5 inches.

Why is acupuncture and acupressure helpful for some people? According to Robert O. Becker, research professor and medical investigator at Upstate Medical Center, Syracuse, New York, the meridian system is more primitive than and to some degree *independent* of the nervous system. The prime function of the system is that of sensing injury and effecting repair. Other studies show that acupuncture works by causing release of endorphins, natural opiates that bind to receptors and suppress pain signal transmission to the brain and produce descending nerve signals. Its success also depends apparently on changes in energy fields and electrical circuits that flow in the body. Journals including the *American Journal of Acupuncture* and *Acupuncture and Electro-therapeutics Research* carry ongoing research reports.

Possible side effects of acupuncture are those associated with any injection: fainting, bleeding under the skin, and infection due to improper sterilization. Acupuncture is not recommended for those with abnormally slow clotting time for the blood, those who are pregnant (acupuncture may start labor pains), and those with certain skin conditions.

The National Council of Acupuncture Schools and Colleges now has 12 members and is seeking accreditation for programs. The American Academy of Acupuncture provides lawmakers and medical specialty boards with advice.

Faith Healers. I had been in practice for over 30 years before I went to a faith healing service. A nationally known healer, Joe Williams, was in Minneapolis, and I was invited to attend a healing service. After it was over, I met the kindly, vibrant, 80-year-old Pentecostal preacher who had traveled the world using his "gift" of healing in his Christian ministry. Brother Williams and I "hit it off" from the start, and that marked the beginning of my studies of faith healing. They took me to Oral Roberts University School of Medicine in Tulsa and many other places.

I found that faith healing is indigenous to all countries throughout the world. It has existed for at least 4000 years, and it is not the monopoly of any one religion. Although certain "healers" such as Olga Worrall and her husband, Ambrose, of Baltimore, seem to have more of a proclivity for this skill, healing, I found, is a natural human attribute for a surprising number of people.

Researchers in the field claim that there is an energy force that travels in waves and is part of the concept in "energy medicine." People who are natural sources of this energy and sympathetic by nature can become healers. Other individuals are "drainers" of this energy or energy force. Nurses and other care givers report such draining effects from patients as one of the causes of emotional fatigue which can even cause "stress burnout."

A number of professional associations have been developed around persons interested in faith healing. These include the Association for Research and Enlightenment (ARE), Spiritual Frontiers Fellowship, Life Energies, Inc., the Academy of Parapsychology and Medicine, and the Order of St. Luke the Physician.

In Great Britain, healers outnumber the practitioners of all the alternative therapies. There are about 55,000 orthodox medical practitioners and 20,000 faith healers. Organizations active there include the National Federation of Spiritual Healers, British Alliance of Healers Association, and the Churches' Fellowship of Healing.

Clinical Ecology. This field began with the work of the allergist Dr. Herbert Rinkel and is concerned about the effects that foods and various chemicals in the air, water, and environment have on one's health. A variety of chronic illnesses including depression, alcoholism, migraine, and hypertension are believed to have allergic etiology.

Iridology. Iris diagnosis or iridology is the diagnosis of disease based on observations of the iris of the eye. References to this method are found in the works of the ancient Greek physicians Hippocrates and Phillipus. Modern study began with the work of a Hungarian, Ignatz von Peczely. Each zone of the eye is believed to serve as a mirror to function of organs throughout the body.

Kinesiology. Kinesiology is a technique developed initially by George Goodheart as applied kinesiology and later refined by John Diamond as behavioral kinesiology. It is widely used by chiropractors for allergy testing and involves the testing of the strength of target muscles. The deltoideus muscle of the arm is commonly used.

Macrobiotics. The Japanese philosopher George Ohsawa introduced the term *macrobiotics*. He felt that the term reflected the spirit of what a healthy person should feel: *macro* meaning large or great and *bios* meaning life. Since his death in the mid-1960s, his work has been carried on by Michio Kuchi in the United States. A largely vegetarian diet is both preventive as well as therapeutic, according to its practitioners.

Naturopaths. Naturopathic practitioners use remedies such as herbs, nutrition, exercise, sunlight, and other simple means to restore and maintain health. They reject surgery and drugs except as a last resort. Naturopathy traces its lineage back to ancient Egypt. However, the current system stems primarily from the work of physician Benedict Lust (1872-1945). Lust established the first naturopathic school in the United States.

Orthomolecular Medicine. Orthomolecular is a term originally used by chemist and Nobel Prize-winner Linus Pauling in the 1950s for treatment methods that involve megavitamin therapy, especially Vitamin C. Later Dr. Abram Hofer and Dr. Humphry Osmond used high doses of niacin and B-complex vitamins in treating schizophrenia and other mental illnesses. Now, an increasing number of medical problems, including alcoholism, have been helped with high doses of vitamins and mineral supplements.

Reflexology. Reflexology massage has its origins in China but is known to also have been practiced for centuries by natives in Kenya and by North American Indian tribes. It was first described in U.S. medical journals in the early 1900s as easing the pain of childbirth. It involves gentle stroking of the foot of the patient with the therapist's fingers.

Rolfing. This technique was developed by Ida Rolf in the 1930s in the United States. It is sometimes called structural processing, postural release, or structural dynamics. It is based on the concept that distortions of normal function of organs and skeletal muscles occur throughout life and are accentuated by the effects of gravity on the body. Rolfing methods help the individual to achieve balance and improved posture.

Shiatsu. *Shiatsu*, in Japanese, means "finger pressure" and involves firm pressure to various points along the same meridian paths used in acupuncture. Shiatsu has been used as a simple home treatment in the Orient for centuries to relieve pain and common ills.

Therapeutic Nutrition. This field of nutrition has its roots in California and its practitioners advocate much more aggressive use of vitamins and mineral supplements than mainstream nutritionists and dieticians.

A maverick medic speaks out

For most of my medical career I was an A.M.A. loyalist. I even developed a homecoming float in college with this prize-winning theme: "If an apple a day keeps the doctor away—then we'll have them *banned* by the A.M.A.!" I wrote for the *Journal of the Student AMA* and started a chapter for the organization at Case Western Reserve in Cleveland. I was a dues-paying member of the county, state, and national organizations in Nebraska and Virginia. Until the last few years I was on one of the review committees of the *Journal of the American Medical Association.*

I can still remember the rift I felt between traditional and nontraditional practitioners—the chiropractors, osteopaths, and naturopaths. It was "Us versus Them," the "Enlightened against the Unenlightened." While working as a young physician in York, Nebraska, in 1954, I was incensed when another doctor accused me of being "friendly" to the local chiropractors.

This was the Golden Age of Medicine. We physicians who practiced in the 1950s and '60s had everything going for us—powerful antibiotics, new tranquilizers, and remarkable blood pressure medications. We had cortisone and ACTH for arthritis. Such tools, coupled with better hospitals and technical resources, gave us power and prestige and prosperity. The 1970s were even better with the addition of computers, space-age technology, bigger hospitals, new surgical techniques, and more potent medications. There was certainly no reason for the M.D.s to look for alternatives.

Why, then, did I, an orthodox M.D., become in the 1970s a medical maverick? Why did I start talking to nontraditional practitioners? Why did I begin to break away from the A.M.A. herd?

It all started when I began listening, truly listening, to the people who registered for my "Course for Activated Patients." I heard people saying unpleasant things about the practice of medicine, such as: "My doctor is more interested in tests than in me." "My obstetrician never listens to me." "The hospitals are too big." "Medicine is like a big machine or a big factory." "I know what's best for my children." "Do the doctors have to do things in such a uniform, impersonal way?" "I'm not just a number."

As I traveled about the United States I started making it a point wherever I was to talk with all kinds of health workers. In 1982 I joined the American Academy of Medical Preventics (AAMP), a group of 1000 or more physicians interested in chelation therapy, nutrition, and various alternatives in preventive medicine. It was with AAMP that I also found something I had never experienced before—legal harassment for physicians and others involved with nontraditional medicine.

Such harassment has a long history. In the mid-19th century about 80% of the physicians in America were allopaths, 15% were homeopaths, and 5% eclectics who used botanical medicines. By the time of the Civil War, the physicians who eventually formed the American Medical Association decided to eliminate the competition and began in the northeastern states of the United States to persuade the state legislators that there was a distinct difference between the allopaths and the others.

In those years, most physicians went to medical school, but an appreciable number received their training from preceptors who were practicing physicians.

The A.M.A. formed political coalitions over the years and by World War I had convinced the Rockefeller Foundation and the Carnegie Foundation to evaluate medical education. This led to the Flexner Report (named after Abraham Flexner from Johns Hopkins who chaired the group making the report). The report said that local physicians acting as preceptors were not an efficient way to train doctors and that Johns Hopkins-type schools and hospitals with full-time faculty and four-year curricula were required. The foundations then pumped money into the schools that fit this model and those that didn't fell onto hard times and most eventually ceased operations.

The A.M.A. then convinced most legislators by the 1930s that licensing boards were necessary to distinguish between the properly trained and those who weren't.

Then in the 1950s the American public gradually lost the desire to even question the doctor as to what would be done with their health care. This transition resulted clearly from the ability of the A.M.A. to gain autonomy and complete authority over the practice of medicine.

Recent developments, however, show that the orthodox physicians who control the political machinery affecting licensure are not going to be able to interfere with medical practice at *their* whim or will. Legal forces protect physicians—not just by guarding them from outside scrutiny—but in *limiting* the way the orthodox can adversely affect them by "judging" their practice—through the political boards of medical examiners— by getting at patient records or other investigative means.

Legal and economic barriers in the United States currently limit access for most Americans to alternative therapies, but the pendulum of political control has begun to swing away from the medical establishment. In Europe, for example, the University of Paris states that medical students there receive training in homeopathy, osteopathy, acupuncture, and a variety of other healing modalities. Major insurance companies in the Netherlands now reimburse policy owners for a variety of alternative therapies, and the Dutch government has nine commissions investigating the efficacy of the therapies. Great Britain and Canada have similar plans. Closer to home, the Office of Technology Assessment, a branch of Congress, has assembled several dozen research and clinical specialists to brainstorm ways to evaluate alternative therapies.

With the current power in the hands of the medical establishment, most physicians stay in line. If they don't they are subjected to a carefully orchestrated hassling process. This can consist of investigators from the medical licensing board calling the physicians and patients and issuing legal orders for clinical records, printing adverse reports in the county medical society newsletters and encouraging censure by the membership committee, refusing payment for medical insurance claims, and removing hospital privileges.

The ultimate weapon is the threat by the state medical board to remove the physician's means of livelihood—the medical license. Under current legislation this can be done in a *closed meeting*.

Physicians who choose to practice maverick medicine therefore must follow a thin gray line of compliance and are frightened away from some nontraditional methods.

A legal ruling in 1985 could diminish the A.M.A.'s control, through direct and indirect political activity, of the state boards of medical licensure. The South Carolina Supreme Court has "struck down" the way doctors discipline doctors in their state. The Court said the Board of Medical Examiners is unconstitutionally composed "in the medical disciplinary function" because its members are drawn exclusively from the ranks of the South Carolina Medical Association. Membership in that organization, an affiliate of the A.M.A., is a prerequisite for serving on the Board.

If pushed far enough, doctors can resort to state or federal courts, but such a decision can represent a cost of $50,000 and many months—even years—of emotional turmoil for these physicians and their families.

How does a person choose an alternative?

With that professional view of the often rocky road of alternative therapy, what is the average lay person to do when faced with hard questions:

- What do I do when my M.D. finds out I went to an acupuncturist and throws a royal fit?
- If I choose an alternative health worker, how do I avoid getting ripped off or know how to sort out the good from the bad?

First, as for the M.D. who throws the royal fit, remember that your physician is a professional resource for you like a lawyer or an architect. The physician does not "own" you. This is the day of consumer preference. Not everyone drives a BMW and even Coca Cola is subjected to the Pepsi challenge!

Second, in this day of increased public knowledge, do your homework on the alternative therapy. Visit the office of the practitioner. Ask to see articles and reprints on the therapy and visit with patients who receive care at the facility. Inquire about the training of the health worker and professional membership. If you don't feel comfortable about what you see and hear, do some more checking. Trust your intuitive hunches.

In today's medical scene the traditional practitioners are still in control, but in my opinion, are losing ground. There are many reasons for this change. Marilyn Ferguson had this to say: "Yesterday's quackery is today's doctrine. ... What is proper licensure and control? ... Should the public be protected from acupuncturists, midwives, herbalogists, biofeedback trainers, homeopaths? ... Should the public not also be protected from dubious surgery and freely prescribed Valium?" *(Journal of Holistic Medicine,* Fall/Winter 1981).

After three decades of medical practice and research, I believe that health is not something obtained just through pills, penicillin, pollution control, or psychotherapy. Health is not deliverable only by the A.M.A.—or for that matter only by the people in different hats. We need health care professionals of all kinds to assist us in recovery from ills and injuries and to teach us to prevent as many problems as possible. The underlying reality is that health is a God-given blessing, and each of us has the responsibility to improve it and protect it!

NINECHAPTER NINE

Big Changes Ahead— Will You Be Ready?

- **Americans Growing Older Says Bureau**
- **How Doctors Cause Disease**
- **High Tech or Low Tech?**
- **Patient Days Down; Workers Being Laid Off**
- **Federal Cuts in Budget Decried**
- **Church Announces Healing Ministry**

What do these diverse headlines have in common? Why have doctors fallen in the public's esteem? What services formerly provided by the government should be offered by the private sector? What role can churches play in the future of health care?

The graying of America

A recent survey of the members in my local congregation showed that the average age of the membership was 51. The U.S. Census Bureau announced the same week that about 30% of Americans are now *over 50* years of age. By the end of

132

this decade there will be 31.8 million Americans over the age of 65. Never before in the history of the world has a nation had to face the circumstance in which there were so many elders. This evidence of the "Graying of America" has profound implications not only for the future of health care but also for housing, nutrition, clothing, recreation, education, travel, and a wide array of religious, social, and political issues.

With the rapid growth of the "50-plus" sector of the American public comes a whole new spectrum of health problems. In 1934 chronic illness accounted for 30% of all illnesses, while today they account for more than 80%—and most of these are associated with problems found in later life. A study in 1975 showed that arthritis, coronary artery disease, cardiovascular diseases which diminish circulation to the brain and legs, and similar chronic conditions accounted for 63% of all physicians' visits and 72% of all brief hospital admissions. It also showed that people 65-69 years of age average about three hospital days per year while individuals over 80 average 8.3 days.

Other reports state that over $30 billion is spent on health care for the elderly, with an average per-capita cost for older persons of $1,360, of which 70% is spent on hospital and nursing-home care. In another study, the average out-of-pocket health expenses for elderly citizens totalled $613, approximately 11% of their income.

When Medicare was passed by Congress in 1966, it was provided as a program to help alleviate high costs of medical care for senior citizens. Now, however, with extended care benefits and home

care limited to 100 days, hospital benefits restrict-
ed to 90 days (if the reserve pool of 60 days has
been exhausted), deductible and coinsurance payments being increased, and other measures to save
federal dollars, the elderly are now paying *more*
for health care than before the passage of the Medicare Act. It is not surprising then that medical
costs are the leading cause of poverty in later life!

In addition to these economic factors, another
wide range of barriers are imposed on our elders.
These are in many ways as bad—maybe worse—
as the financial ones:

- Payment systems that encourage institutionali-
  zation rather than nursing care in the home or
  homemaker services (e.g., insurance companies
  will pay $400 per day for hospital care but only
  $100-$150 for in-the-home care).
- Lack of hospice services to provide care and support for patients afflicted with terminal illnesses
  as an alternative to the impersonal services in
  the usual large, complex, and expensive hospitals.
- Shortages of physicians and primary-care practitioners in poverty areas of inner cities and rural
  areas, where a significant number of the elderly
  live.
- The demise of the general practitioner—the
  most familiar medical resource for older persons—with the result that many people get lost
  in the health-care system because they become
  confused or simply lack the stamina and so-
  phistication to negotiate through the maze.

- Negative attitudes and prejudices against older people by health-care professionals, society at large, and older citizens themselves.
- A society that imposes high technology options on us—with a high price tag and often a narrow margin of safety—with the assumption that more is better.

Selfcare options offered

Because of these economic factors and other barriers, we can no longer assume that we can solve health-care problems with the methods we now use. Limits may have to be imposed on the costs and numbers of organ transplants and coronary bypasses that we can provide and pay for. We may have to work on some new assumptions. Perhaps less is better in many ways. We may have to get along with the existing technological, financial, and medical resources. There may be dramatically different roles and methods needed for both professionals and laity.

One method that has been proposed is that of greatly increased selfcare and home-care resources. A recent study by a major market research firm resulted in a 300-page report on programs, products, services, and resources that are now available.* It showed, among other things, the relative costs of selfcare versus professional care. This is an area that can create substantial changes in the economics of health care.

*Frost and Sullivan, Inc., 106 Fulton Street, New York NY 10038. "Home Healthcare Products and Services in the U.S." (212) 233-1080.

Such programs help educate elderly people about their health, methods of prevention, and the health-care system. They can give the elderly the confidence to be more assertive with professionals, counselors, managers, politicians, and all the other people involved with the health-care system.

A major premise of selfcare is increased individual responsibility for one's own health and that of your family members. Individuals in selfcare and self-help groups share a common condition and come together to offer one another the benefit of mutual experiences, support, and advice. Gartner and Riessman reported that in 1977 there were 15 million Americans involved in half-a-million self-help groups and that these numbers have grown rapidly since then. Some of the better known groups reported include Alcoholics Anonymous, Weight Watchers, and Reach for Recovery. Such groups do work that is divided into four categories: (1) Rehabilitative work, (2) Behavioral change, (3) Primary care, (4) Prevention.

Several innovative programs have been developed that focus on the health of elders. These include "Growing Younger" (Healthwise, Inc., Boise ID 83701), "A Healthy Old Age" (Health Promotion with the Elderly Project, School of Social Work, University of Washington, Seattle WA 98195), and "Elderplan's Self-Care Program" (Metropolitan Jewish Geriatric Center, Brooklyn NY 11219).

Diseases doctors cause

Norman Cousins, adjunct professor at the U.C.L.A. School of Medicine, editor, author, and popular lecturer, has described how physicians' attitudes, words, and the way they communicate them affect the healing process. In an interview with Tom Ferguson, M.D. ("How Doctors Cause Disease," *Medical Self-Care*, Winter 1983, pp. 12-19), Cousins described his own experiences as a patient and as that of a member of the Department of Psychiatry and Behavioral Sciences. He pointed out that when words such as *cancer* and *heart attack* are used by a doctor, the patient can process them into fear or panic. Fear constricts blood vessels. This reduces blood flow and makes it difficult for the different systems of the body to function. The human brain in turn ("the most prolific gland in the human body") finds it difficult to secrete substances that allow the body to alleviate pain, combat infection, and fortify the immune system.

Cousins reported, "The idea of psychological iatrogenesis is nothing new—it's as old as Hippocrates, the father of medicine himself. If asked to share his most important teaching, he would probably have reported his favorite maxim as:

" *'Primum non nocere,'* he told them, 'First do no harm.' He instructed young doctors to pay very close attention to the way the body could heal itself, and he warned them that they must be very careful to do nothing to interfere with that process but to do all they could to help it along. 'The body is the physician of its own diseases.'"

High tech versus low tech

Each spring students of the Humanistic Health Committee at the University of Minnesota sponsor a program about a controversial topic. The planning committee asked me to present the negative aspects of problems associated with high technology. The program was called "Whither Goeth Medicine?" and they asked me to debate Dr. John Najarian, chairman of the Department of Surgery at the School of Medicine, who would defend high technology.

So on the day of the debate I arrived at the huge lecture hall and found it packed with students, faculty, and curious folks from the university. I mused as I looked up at the sea of faces surrounding me in the amphitheater. The majority of the audience either earned their living providing high tech medicine—or were being trained to do so— and must have wondered what in the world I would say. I thought, "Now I know how the Christians in Rome felt before the lions came in!"

When my opponent arrived he was trailed by a whole retinue of resident surgeons and other assistants direct from the surgery, still wearing green scrub suits. After introductions, "the debate" began. Najarian extolled the virtues and marvels of transplants and heart-lung pumps and computers and the antirejection drug, cyclosporine.

When my turn came, I pointed out that far too many Americans are becoming alienated from today's medical world. With the huge institutions that have been spawned by science, technology, and complex business and economic forces, physicians interact only briefly with patients and rely on increasingly complex equipment, surgical procedures, and batteries of biomedical tests.

The cries I hear are, "No one would listen to me"; "I was afraid of all those X-rays"; "I didn't want them to crack open my husband's chest because I knew what happened to my brother after his bypass operation!"

I told the audience about a study at the University of Colorado of 23 families who requested low tech options instead of the high tech ones offered as a part of their routine medical services. When asked why, the researchers were told:

1. They were frustrated with or distrusted standard medical intervention with surgery and drugs.
2. The individuals had a desire for more "natural" approaches to health care.
3. They had faith in nonmedical approaches based on religious and cultural reasons.

Another study I reported to the students and faculty had come from the University of Texas—Galveston Branch. It showed that many people are not going to the big medical complexes but are seeking care in other nontraditional settings. These were described as:

1. *Whole Person/Holistic Health*
   Such facilities are smaller and more personalized, where patients feel they are part of a caring community that preserves privacy and the autonomy of each patient.

2. *High-Level Wellness*
   These centers emphasize personal growth and self-development, as well as traditional medical

and diagnostic services. They usually combine cardiovascular testing with fitness training, stress management, and nutritional counseling.

3. *Esoteric/Unconventional Healing*

These organizations offer a wide variety of modalities such as yoga, acupuncture and acupressure, rolfing, homeopathy, chiropractic services, herbal medicine, kinesiology, paraelectricity treatments, and other therapy and methods not used or accepted by the medical establishment.

I also expressed my opinion that far too many modern "high-tech docs" have forgotten that the margin of safety for their procedures is far too narrow.

I urged more "high touch" was needed in the "high-tech" hospitals and closed my remarks with the words of the Scottish poet, Robert Burns:

"You take the high road and I'll take the low road,
And I'll get to Scotland before you!"

The students gave me a rousing ovation, but, I'm sorry to say, I don't think the surgeons in the audience heard my message or changed their minds about high technology.

Future directions

Now, with that background on the "Graying of America," the perverse economics of sickness care, the high cost and narrow safety of high-tech care, the changing role of doctors and patients on today's medical scene, I'd like to look at some future directions for health care.

Those readers who know of my many years of work with "Activated Patients" and medical self-care might appreciate a remark made by Fred Pearman, Ph.D., director of education at the BioGenesis Medical Center near Oklahoma City. When I shared with him some of the things I was planning for this book, he predicted that lay persons will have an expanded role in health care. He remarked, "I think we will see ACTS-tivated Christians."

At first I didn't catch what he said, so he repeated the phrase, "You'll see ACTS-tivated Christians. I use that term because the book of Acts has so many spirit-filled stories that involved health (e.g., Acts 3:9—the beggar who had been crippled for 40 years and regained full use of his legs; Acts 6:8—the miracles performed by Stephen; Acts 9:36-43—the recovery of Dorcas.)"

Many new healing ministries in churches and religious organizations are begun each year. This is because the very essence of the church is to be a healing community. In *The Church Is Healing*, Michael Wilson wrote, "It should be as absurd to think about a congregation's ministry *without* healing as it would be to think of Christ's ministry without it!"

Many people, however, for a number of reasons, have semantic hang-ups when they think of "healing" ministries:

- Some automatically think of "healing" only in the framework of faith-healing of people such as Oral Roberts, the television evangelist.

- Some think of it as something supernatural.
- Others might think of the healings of Christian Science practitioners and feel uncomfortable about the results attributed to them.
- Still others associate it with the charismatic movement and feel it is somehow alien to their mainline churches.

Whatever one's hang-ups may be, however, recent changes in federal and state fiscal policies will make big changes in our local resources for health and social services. The "safety net" for poor people, elderly people, and people with handicapping conditions is no longer present in many communities. Political observers predict there will be even less services in the future. It is my opinion that local churches and volunteer organizations in our cities will be asked to provide an increasing amount of such health and social services.

Churches as caring communities are already active in providing a variety of such services. Some are already actively involved in health care. An increasing number of church leaders both on the local and national scene realize that most illness in our society can be prevented particularly if discovered in its early stages. The congregational setting lends itself well to picking up early cries for help through prayer chains and general awareness of personal circumstances.

Physicians, nurses, and other professionals realize the spiritual dimensions of much disease and know that each of us can—indeed must—play a greater role in keeping people healthy spiritually. In order to accomplish this we need to develop specific ways of increasing the awareness of the average church or synagogue member about the importance of one's faith in maintaining good health.

One way to do this has been developed by Evangelical Health Systems of Oak Park, Illinois. This organization, working under Granger and H. Jill Westberg and the Lutheran General Hospital of Park Ridge, Illinois, has created a model program called "Nurses in Our Churches." Qualified nurses skilled in whole person medicine, health education, and personal health counseling have been placed on church staffs.

This model focuses on parishes as health agencies and has created the concept of using nurses as "Ministers of Health" in the same way we have used other professionals as Ministers of Music and Ministers of Christian Education for many years. Each congregation forms a health committee to assist the nurse in formulating policies, giving support, and coordinating the work of the nurse. A community physician serves as a backup and professional resource to the Minister of Health. The nurses are given training in methods and materials used. The benevolence budget of the church plus special gifts from members and organizations serves as the source for funds.

Another excellent model is the Open Door for Shepherds that has been developed by a congregation in Golden Valley, Minnesota. It involves several hundred volunteers who are alerted to people who are experiencing events such as graduation, marriage, birth of a child, new homesite, new membership in the church, anniversaries, sickness and

injury, career change, loss of job, unusual achieve-
ment, retirement, entering nursing home, grief and
loss. With the help of a full-time coordinator, the
volunteers are trained to visit their fellow Christians. The tools they use as shepherds are support,
love, and concern. The program has brought im-
pressive results and made the congregation strong
and dynamic.

The role of Christians for the rest of the 20th
century can perhaps be described in words from
the hymn, "Just As I Am."

> In sickness, sorrow, want, or care,
> Each other's burdens help us share;
> May we, where help is needed, there
> Give help as though to you.

There are big changes ahead—come join us and
get ready!

CHAPTER TEN

The Selfcare Guide

In the most extensive, controlled selfcare study yet reported, Donald Vickery and researchers at Rhode Island Group Health Association found significant *decreases* in total medical visits and minor visits that averaged 17% and 35% respectively when persons were given selfcare training.

A study conducted by Donald Kemper for a health maintenance organization in Boise, Idaho, showed that those patients who received selfcare training found their medical costs were 13% lower than a similar group which did not receive training.

Martin Evers developed a selfcare educational program and ran a controlled study of several hundred Blue Cross/Blue Shield enrollees in Dayton, Ohio. The experimental group which took a selfcare course found that their costs went *down* $38 per family while the control group found their costs went *up* $21 during the same period of time.

My studies at Georgetown University and recent ones in a number of employee groups in Minnesota showed that selfcare training helps individuals decrease the number of doctor visits by 10% to 25%.

Programs such as these and others have enhanced the capabilities of lay persons to do for themselves *with training* what people have always done *without training* in handling common health problems. Although some skeptics view such training as an effort to take traditional duties *away* from professionals, selfcare should be considered *part* of the health care system and is neither opposed to nor the same as professional care.

If a lay person institutes proper measures such as prompt bandaging of a cut finger, effective handling of a case of diarrhea, or other steps described in this chapter, the body will quickly heal. Normal function will be restored in a short time in the vast majority of people.

It is only when an individual does "dumb things" or, through ignorance, uses methods that may interfere with normal healing, that complications can develop. It is then that professional assistance is needed. Should "get professional help if" instructions appear, *seek professional care promptly!* If such instructions are not listed, follow the guide and institute the plan described. You are then practicing *selfcare*.

The SOAP Selfcare System

The information in this chapter is based on the SOAP System, a method developed by the Sehnert Selfcare Network. It can be used by individuals for themselves or their families in solving problems associated with everyday ills and injuries. It is an integral part of the educational programs that have been offered since 1970 to thousands of activated patients, their spouses, employees and other interested persons.

The goals of the Network have been to help participants:

1. Accept more individual responsibility for their own health care and that of their families.

2. Learn skills of observation, description, and handling of common illnesses, injuries, and emergencies.

3. Increase their basic knowledge about health promotion methods that will improve the health status of persons who use them.

4. Understand how to use health care resources, personnel, services, insurance, and medication more economically and appropriately.

SOAP has its origins in the problem-oriented medical record developed by Lawrence Weed, M.D., at the University of Vermont in the early 1970s and now used by students, nurses, and physicians in most medical schools and hospitals as an effective way to keep clinical records.

The acronym SOAP comes from four words: *S*ubjective, *O*bjective, *A*ssessment, and *P*lan. By following this sequence in evaluating frequently occurring health problems, you will be able to handle them without panic. Use of the SOAP System helps you *gain* skills, insight, and confidence and enables you to *save* time, worry, and money. It will assist you in home treatment of *common* ailments and tell you when to seek professional help with *uncommon* ones.

SOAP. By following these steps in the SOAP review you can be more efficient at gathering information and forming your health care plan.

S **subjective information:** Ask questions such as, How do you feel? What bothers you most? Are there other factors, such as stress or lack of rest?

O **objective information:** Collect specific information such as your temperature, pulse rate, condition of your throat, signs of swelling or discoloration.

A **assessment:** Put the subjective and objective information together, using "The Selfcare Guide."

P **plan:** What will you do? Are there "get professional help" signals? What is your home care plan? List specifics and a deadline for improvement.

Step 1—subjective information

The first step in the SOAP System involves *describing* the symptoms associated with the problem. You will learn to develop a medical history by asking what, when, and where questions about the illness, injury, or emergency confronting you or someone you might be helping.

This is done by increasing your awareness of symptoms and learning to describe the signals that the body sends out when a dysfunction or disorder is present. Such signals are in some ways similar to the red lights, dials, and buzzers in your car that inform you of the status of gasoline, oil, brakes, and so on. Symptoms "talk" to you and even give you "advice." (They are not things you should hide with a lot of aspirin or other pain medication!)

The body gives us "bad signals" such as pain, distress, and fatigue as well as "good signals" such as satisfaction after a healthy meal, relaxation during play with a child or pet and exhilaration after vigorous exercise or a refreshing night's sleep.

In "The Selfcare Guide" common symptoms are clearly listed, for example, under earache (see p. 196) you will find "aching/pain/sound in ear, chills or fever, dizziness," and so on. Compare your symptoms with those listed.

Step 2—objective information

The second step in SOAP involves *measuring* and observing clinical events. Such things as the temperature, pulse, blood pressure, and respiration rate give you readings about the status of your health and are called vital signs. Examples of other observations that you can count or measure in some way include the number of diarrhea movements in say, one hour, the length of the cut in your leg, the number of times you got up at night to urinate, and so on.

People need a certain number of "tools" to effectively do some of this measuring. You can buy such tools or medical equipment from mail order catalog companies and retail stores (drug, health food, and full-line department stores). Here are some supplies you should have:

Family black bag—A complete kit of equipment includes an otoscope, stethoscope, sphygmomanometer, thermometer, high intensity penlight, and instructions for the use of the instruments. A complete kit costs from $85 to $120.

Stethoscope—for checking heart sounds, blood pressure, breathing sounds. Stethoscopes cost about $10 to $12. Sources are some drug stores and chain stores. Another source is Self-Care Catalog (P.O. Box 1000, Pt. Reyes CA 94956).

Sphygmomanometer—for measuring blood pressures. They are available as aneroid (dial) or electronic units. Costs vary, depending on the unit: aneroid unit—$27.50 to $50; electronic unit—$49 to $220. Sources are full-line department stores, drugstores, and catalog firms.

Otoscope—for looking inside ears. The cost ranges from $17.95 (Earscope available from Self-Care Catalog) to about $70.

Thermometer—for taking temperature. Use rectal thermometer for children, oral for adults. Thermometers cost under $2 and are available at any drugstore.

Penlight—for examining throat, ears, nose. A disposable penlight costs about six for $3 and can be found in some retail stores.

Taking your temperature

Your temperature is a measure of the balance between heat production and loss in your body. Exercise, shivering, muscle tension, infection, and external warmth produce heat and make your temperature rise. Sweating, panting, fatigue, and external cold draw heat away and lower your temperature.

The purpose of taking your body temperature is to determine if the balance of your heat production and loss is stable. In a healthy person, this would be an oral temperature of 98.6° F. (37° C.), though there are variations in "normal" temperatures. Several factors that affect temperatures are:

- *Time of day.* Temperatures are lower in the morning, higher in the late afternoon.
- *Age.* Infants (older than three weeks) and children have a slightly higher normal reading.
- *Emotions.* When you get "hot under the collar," your body temperature is likely to rise in anticipation of action.
- *The site where the temperature is taken.* Rectal temperatures are routinely 1° higher than oral and 2° higher than axillary (armpit) temperatures.
- *Illness from infection.* The body kills germs with higher temperatures.

See page 154 for directions on taking temperatures.

Taking your pulse

Each time the heart pumps blood out of itself into the cardiovascular system, a pulse wave is generated (like the ripple that is generated on the water surface when you throw a stone into a pond). You can feel this pulse wave in places where your arteries come close to the surface of your skin.

The purpose of taking your pulse is to determine how fast your heart is beating (i.e., pumping). Common sites to take your pulse are at your wrist, forehead, and the carotid area of your neck (near your jawbone). The usual rate is from 60-80 pulses a minute, though variations are caused by several factors:

- *Age.* Children have higher pulse rates.
- *Exercise.* Your pulse speeds up after exertion as your heart pumps faster to meet increased demands for oxygen.
- *Emotions and pain.* Both raise your pulse.
- *Fever.* Your pulse will rise when you have a fever.
- *Time of day.* Pulses are slower in the morning and faster later in the day.

See page 155 for directions on taking pulses.

Taking your respiration rate

The rate at which you breathe helps to indicate how much oxygen you need—either how hungry your cells are for it or how efficiently you process it to get it to them. It's extremely variable, as you know from thinking about how slowly a person breathes when asleep compared to how fast a person pants after terrific exertion. These factors also affect respiration rates:

- *Your emotional state* (agitation, from good or bad causes, will speed up respiration).
- *The presence of such conditions as asthma or chronic pulmonary disease,* which decrease efficiency and raise the rate to compensate.
- *Smoking habits* (smokers breathe more quickly because their lungs are less efficient).

THE SELFCARE GUIDE

- *Level of physical fitness* (lung efficiency increases with improved conditioning).
- *The presence of a fever* (the typical feverish child will breathe much more quickly than normally).

See page 156 for directions on taking respiration rates.

Taking your blood pressure

Blood pressure is the force your heart exerts on your blood to force it through the cardiovascular system in your body. The heart squeezes (contracts) and pushes blood through your arteries and veins to carry oxygen and nutrients to (and wastes away from) all parts of your body.

Blood pressure is measured in terms of the millimeters of mercury it can push up when a cuff is wrapped tightly around a main artery. Using a cuff, you can measure both the systolic (heart contracted) and diastolic (heart relaxed) pressures. They are expressed as a ratio of systolic to diastolic pressure.

The normal range for systolic pressure is 100-145 millimeters of mercury; the normal range for diastolic pressure is 60-90. Several factors can influence your blood pressure:

- Emotional state related to stressful events in life.
- Cigarette and smoking habits.
- Amount of coffee (or caffeine-containing drinks such as tea, cola drinks) consumed each day.
- Level of physical fitness.
- Amount of salt used in food.

See page 157 for directions on taking blood pressure.

How to take temperatures

Oral temperature

Note: Readings will be inaccurate if the person has had something to drink in the last 15 minutes.

1. Shake mercury level down to below 98.6° F. (37°C.).
2. Insert thermometer under person's tongue.
3. Ask the person to close mouth and breathe through nose.
4. Take thermometer out after three minutes.
5. Read highest level of mercury; record reading.

Rectal temperature

Note: Temperatures from rectal readings will be 1° higher than others.

1. Shake mercury level down to below 98.6° F. (37° C.).
2. Lubricate bulb with vaseline jelly.
3. Insert the bulb and no more than 1½ inches of the stem into the person's anus.
4. Take thermometer out after two minutes.
5. Wipe off thermometer and read highest level of mercury; record reading.

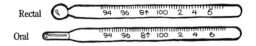

Axillary (armpit) temperature

Note: This method is less accurate than the two methods above.

Same method as oral procedure above, but place the bulb on the skin under the person's armpit and keep it in place for five minutes.

How to take pulses

Note: It is best to take your pulse while you are at rest, sitting in a comfortable position. You will need a watch with a second hand.

Wrist site
1. Lay your index and middle fingers across the inner surface of your wrist, about an inch from the base of your thumb.
2. Locate the pulse there (the radial artery pulse). Count the beats for 15 seconds, and multiply by four for the rate per minute.

Neck site
1. Tip head to side and tuck index and middle fingers under the angle of your jawbone.
2. Straighten up your head and locate the pulse (the carotid artery pulse). Count the beats for 15 seconds, and multiply by four for the rate per minute.

Forehead site
1. Put your index and middle fingers along your hairline, about halfway between your ear and eyebrow.
2. Locate the pulse (the temporal artery pulse). Count the beats for 15 seconds, and multiply by four for the rate per minute.

How to take respiration rates

The respiration rate is not as important as the other vital signs, but may provide useful information, particularly for asthma and emphysema victims. Here's how you determine it—it's very nearly impossible to take your own!

1. Ask the person to sit upright or in a semi-upright position in a chair or bed.
2. Make sure that the normal breathing motion of the chest is not obscured with clothing or bedding.
3. Gently place the palm of your hand on the person's chest. (Put thumb in notch between collar bones on midline of chest.) Watch your hand move with each breath.
4. Count number of breaths in one minute. (Normal respiration rate is 12-14 breaths/minute.)

How to take blood pressures

1. Have the person sit in a chair with the arm placed on a table or arm rest.
2. Wrap the cuff around the bare arm with the lower edge of the band at the crease where the elbow bends.
3. Place the head of the stethoscope under the cuff. Listen for heart sounds.
4. Inflate the cuff until the heart sounds disappear.
5. Slowly open the valve of the bulb of the sphygmo-manometer until you hear the sounds again. Note the reading (e.g., 130).
6. Release the valve completely and let the air out of the balloon within the interior of the cuff. Note the reading when the heart sounds disappear (e.g., 80).

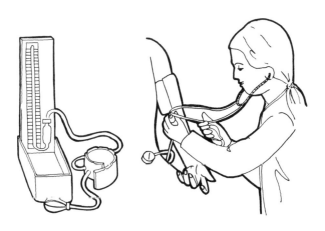

Step 3—assessment

The third step in SOAP involves putting subjective and objective information together and *comparing* or *assessing* it. This is done by recording the subjective conditions and objective findings that are present and placing them on the SOAP Worklist (see p. 166). This process is somewhat like what county tax assessors do when they estimate the taxable value of your home. The assessor compares your home with, for example, other two-story brick houses with attached garage on 100-foot lots, and estimates a value. Your job with health assessment is to compare your situation with the descriptions in this book and determine how close your problem matches it. Then you are ready to start a treatment plan *if* there are no "get professional help" signals present (which indicate possible trouble for a variety of reasons and that selfcare may *not* be indicated!)

Step 4—plan

The fourth and final step involves developing your treatment plan. What will you do? How long should you treat the condition?

Plans involve using certain home care supplies, implementing selected treatment procedures (like applying heat in the form of hot compresses, or bandaging, etc.), or taking over-the-counter medications. It is best to keep medications, supplies, and tools in a single area—most likely you keep them now in your bathroom, but a drawer or linen closet is less exposed to moisture and heat (and is more childproof) and thus is preferable.

Store medications in a lockable cabinet even if you don't have any children around routinely. Near your supplies, post a list of key phone numbers for your doctor, rescue squad, emergency room at the hospital, poison control center, fire and police service, and pharmacy.

Applying Heat

The method you choose for applying heat should suit the part of the body you need to treat. Depending on the problem, you may need to apply moist or dry heat.

Treatment	Procedure
Hot compress for back, joints, limbs 	• Wet a large towel thoroughly in warm water; wring it out and fold in thirds lengthwise. Wrap it around or across the affected area. • Repeat twice daily. • Other methods are Cold Comfort (3M) for both heat and cold, or a warm heating pad.
Hot compress for ears	• Soak paper towels in hot water; wring dry. Stuff towels into a small, already-warmed water glass.

SELFCARE/WELLCARE

- Tilt affected ear up and press bottom of glass over ear for 10 minutes.
- Rewarm glass and towels; repeat for another 10 minutes.
- Or try a heating pad or a hot water bottle.

Hot compress for eyes

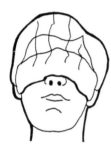

- Soak a washcloth or handkerchief in warm water; wring dry. (Don't use hot water, as it may cause tissue near the eye to swell.)
- Apply once every 3 hours for 5 to 10 minutes.
- Try a cold compress (same method but with cold water) if the eye is swollen or feels itchy.
- Add eye drops after applying these compresses.

Gargle for throats

- Make your own gargle solution: add 1 tsp. of salt to 8 oz. of hot water.
- Gargle once every 2 hours for 5 minutes, until pain ends.
- Or try a hot solution of Cepacol or a similar product available at drugstores.

Hot compress for sinuses

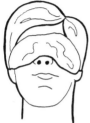

- Soak one towel in hot water; wring dry. Place on forehead or cheeks for 30 seconds.
- Soak another towel in cold water and ice cubes; wring dry. Place on forehead or cheeks for 30 seconds.
- Alternate these hot and cold compresses for 10 minutes.
- Repeat 4 times daily.

Sitz bath for rectums, vaginas

- Fill a tub with enough warm to hot water to cover the buttocks while sitting up.
- Sit in this hot sitz bath for 10 to 15 minutes.

Applying Cold

There are several ways to apply cold to treat injuries and illnesses. Here are several basic procedures.

Treatment	Procedure
Cold compress to control bleeding	• Apply plastic bag filled with crushed ice to the affected area. • Put a popsicle on the cut if it's on a child's lip or cheek. The child will enjoy it—and there's no harm in swallowing a little blood!
Cold soak to treat injured ankles, arms, feet, hands, wrists	• Immerse injured part in bowl, styrofoam cooler, or dishpan filled with cold water (with ice cubes if possible). Soak as needed.
Cold soak to lower fever	• Immerse the person in a tub half-full of tepid water. With a facecloth, drizzle water on back, face and chest; wet hair if practical. • Avoid chilling the person; 20 minutes should be sufficient to lower most fevers. • A shower can be substituted for the tub if necessary. • If the patient can't be bathed, place a plastic sheet or oil cloth under the person and apply cold towels that have been soaked in a solution of 2 quarts water, 1 pint rubbing alcohol, and 1 quart ice cubes.

Cold compress to treat bruises, sinusitis, insect stings	• Put a dozen ice cubes in pan with cold water; soak a towel in it. Wring towel dry and apply to the injured area. Repeat as needed.

Bandages

Bandages keep dirt out of wounds and protect them from further injury. When they cover pads with medication or close cuts, they also promote healing.

Type	Procedure
Basic bandage	• Clean the affected area and control bleeding before applying the bandage. • Use a 2″ x 2″ or 4″ x 4″ sterile gauze dressing or an ouchless bandage (Telfa). • Attach with adhesive tape or roller gauze and tape.
Elastic bandage	• Clean area and apply dressings if needed. • Begin wrapping the area with even, gentle pressure. Do not bind the bandage too tightly! • If you are directed to do so, unwrap the bandage several times a day to relieve the pressure.

Butterfly closure

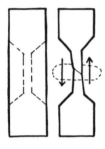

- Use a commercial butterfly closure or make one yourself using ½" adhesive tape.
- Cut the tape as shown; twist one end 360° until both ends have adhesive sides down. Then pull the edges of the wound together and apply.
- Cover with a gauze bandage or Band-Aid (with a large wound you might need to wrap with an elastic gauze bandage).

Bandage removal

- Once a bandage is in place, it's best to leave it on for the first 24 hours. After that, remove and change bandages as often as necessary.
- Soak gauze in cold water before removing to avoid disturbing the wound.
- Remove the bandage lengthwise, as shown, to prevent the wound from reopening.

Splints

Immobilizing an injured part of your body can allow it to heal more quickly in some cases. If you need to splint an extremity, these simple methods will help.

Fingers and toes
Tape fingers or toes to an adjacent finger or toe, with 2 or 3 pieces of ½″-wide tape.

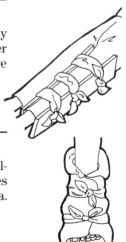

Wrist and forearm
Use a newspaper or magazine to immobilize the injured area, taping it or tying it with pieces of cloth.

Leg
Take 2 boards or pieces of sturdy material and place them on either side of the injured limb. Secure them with cloth pieces or tape.

Ankle
Make a splint with towel or pillow, securing it with tape or pieces of cloth tied around the ankle area.

The SOAP Work List

Subjective Information:

The first step in the SOAP System begins with *describing* the symptoms associated with the problem. Gather as much information or history about how the illness, injury, or problem affects the person or makes them feel. Ask such questions as: "What started the pain?" "Where is the soreness?" "When does the throat hurt most?" or "Why do I sneeze?"

What? _____

When? _____

Where? _____

Objective Information:

The second step in the SOAP System involves *measuring* or making observations about things related to the problem, such as:

Temperature _____   Color of ear drum ___

Blood Pressure _____   Number of times of

Pulse (per minute) __   diarrhea (per hour)

Breathing Rate _____   _____

Color of mucus in   Length of cut/wound

throat _____   (inches) _____

Color of urine _____

Assessment: how to compare *the problem*

The third step in the SOAP System involves comparing the symptoms and observations already made and comparing things about the current problem:

Are the symptoms the same? ___Yes ___No

Are the things you checked or measured the same? ___Yes ___No   If *yes* please list: _____
_____

Have you ever had the problem before?
___Yes ___No   If *yes* please list: _____
_____

Plan: how to plan *and begin treatment (or seek professional help)*

The final step in the SOAP System involves deciding if professional help is, or might be, needed and then begin home treatment plan.

Are there any "Call-the-Professional Signals" present? ___Yes ___No   If *yes* please list: _____
_____

Are the right supplies available for home treatment? ___Yes ___No   If *no* please list what is needed: _____
_____

What is the first treatment to be started? _____

Please describe the plan: _____

When will professional help be obtained if I'm not better? _____

Please set time, circumstances: _____

What's an emergency?

We all recognize that there are emergencies and then there are *emergencies.* A bad fall might leave you with a number of aches and pains— and cause you a good deal of anxiety—but the odds are that you can respond to its effects with informed home care. The conditions below are different, however. If you note any of them, seek medical care *immediately.*

Unconsciousness	When you can't rouse someone, call for help.
Drowsiness (stupor)	When the person is conscious but unable to answer questions, get help. With children and infants, you may need to judge this in contrast with ordinary alertness.
Disorientation	When someone can't remember his or her name, the place or the date (in order of decreasing importance), get help. An injury or illness causing disorientation is serious.
Severe injury	You'll know it when you see it; large wounds, obvious bone fractures, extensive burns need more care than you can give.
Uncontrollable bleeding	Pressure should stop most bleeding; when it fails to, get help. Children cannot afford to lose as much blood as adults can.

Shortness of breath

If a person is unusually short of breath even while resting, and you can rule out hyperventilation, which is most common in young adults, get help.

Severe pain

While pain is subjective, and may be caused by emotional and psychological factors, a person in intense pain still needs relief from it. Don't take pain itself as a barometer of the seriousness of the emergency, but do seek relief from a professional.

How to use the guide

The following "Selfcare Guide" is designed to be self-contained and does not require you to go to outside sources, but a few preliminary comments are necessary to help you use the guide most effectively:

- Flip through the guide, glancing at the large-type headings at the top of the page. Chances are you'll locate the page you need in a few seconds.
- If you are unsure about what your problem is called, check the conditions listed under "Subjective" heading.

ALLERGIC STUFFY NOSE

What you need to know:

Description: Inflammation and congestion of nasal passages caused by allergies to pollen, dust, food and other irritants.
● 10% of population have some kind of nasal allergy each year.
● Minimizing dust and other irritants in rooms, making sure furnace is filtered, and checking to see that air conditioner is clean and working properly may prevent irritation.

Home care supplies:

penlight
antihistamines
oral nasal decongestant

nose drops
glasses of water

SOAP SELFCARE SYSTEM

1 Subjective:

- ● bloody nose
- ● congested nose
- ● coughing
- ● hoarseness
- ● itching eyes, nose
- ● red or watery eyes
- ● sneezing, runny nose
- ● trouble breathing

2 Objective:

● Have assistant examine nasal membranes with penlight. Pale, swollen, waterlogged (sometimes bluish) surface suggests allergy.
● Look for dark circles under child's eyes.
● Keep list of possible irritants.

3 **Assessment:**

- How many subjective conditions are present? _____
- How many objective findings are present? _____

4 **Plan:**

- Take antihistamines or oral nasal decongestant several times a day for no more than 3 days. Then call doctor.
- Rest and stay indoors on windy days.
- Wash hands and face frequently on bad days or in allergy season.
- Use nose drops for relief at bedtime. LIMIT USE TO 3 TIMES A DAY FOR NO MORE THAN 3 DAYS.
- Drink one 8-oz. glass of water per hour to replace fluid lost in nasal discharge.
- Avoid alcohol (a congestant) and stop smoking (an irritant).

Get professional help if:

- Symptoms increase over years and general preventive measures don't help.
- Mucus in nose is thick green or yellow.
- Antihistamines cause drowsiness and it's essential to drive or operate heavy machinery.

ARTHRITIS

What you need to know:

Description: Stiffness and inflammation that usually affect the joints most used but can affect any joint.

● This treatment plan is for common arthritis only.

● Other arthritic conditions are more crippling (rheumatoid arthritis; arthritis due to infection of gout; nonarticular rheumatism, called bursitis or fibrositis) and need professional help.

Home care supplies:

aspirin   Cold Comfort (3M)
heating pad or hot water
  bottle

SOAP Selfcare System

1 Subjective:
- ● aching joints
- ● back, knee, hip pain
- ● bumps in and around joints
- ● dizziness, ringing in ear
- ● limping, trouble walking
- ● loss of appetite
- ● stiff wrist, shoulder, neck
- ● weather causes aching

2 Objective:
- ● Note time of day aching is worst.
- ● Note effect of aspirin.
- ● Examine fingers for knobby areas and bumps (Herberden's nodes) around joints.

3 Assessment:

- How many subjective conditions are present? _____
- How many objective findings are present? _____

4 Plan:

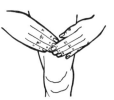

- Apply heat (see p. 159).
- Take aspirin.
- Massage muscles *surrounding* joint (not joint itself) to improve circulation.
- Keep as active as possible to maintain muscle strength (swimming is especially good). If joints are painful, rest after activity.
- Wear extra clothing for warmth in cold weather.

Get professional help if:

- Aspirin causes dizziness, ringing in ears, indigestion, pain in stomach, or constipation.
- Pain is limited to one joint and there is family history of gout.
- General weakness or increasing fatigue develop.

ASTHMA

What you need to know:

Description: A lung condition associated with allergies. Linings of bronchial tubes are inflamed, swollen, and clogged with mucus.

● Asthma distress can be a frightening experience. Keeping calm may reduce the severity of the attack.

● Causes include smoke, dust, pollen, infection, food, medication, exertion, damp weather, emotional stress, fatigue.

Home care supplies:

thermometer
stethoscope
watch with second hand

asthma medication
glasses of water
pillows

SOAP Selfcare System

1 Subjective:
- aching in chest
- breathing pain, wheezing
- congested or runny nose
- coughing, hoarseness
- fever
- shortness of breath
- sleeping
- sneezing

2 Objective:
- Note all possible irritants.
- Note temperature three times daily.
- Check breathing rate at rest (normal is 18-20 breaths/minute for adults).
- Check pulse rate at rest (normal is 68-72 beats/minute for adults).

3 **Assessment:**
- How many subjective conditions are present? _____
- How many objective findings are present? _____

4 **Plan:**
- Follow suggested allergy prevention techniques (see page 171).
- Start asthma medication as soon as possible; continue until wheezing stops.
- DO NOT USE SPRAY FORMS OF ASTHMA MEDICATION WITHOUT MEDICAL ADVICE. They may worsen asthma.
- Use pillows to prop up patient.
- Drink one 8-oz. glass of water, juice, or tea every hour.
- Avoid all known irritants.
- If child develops stomachaches from swallowing large amounts of mucus, help child to vomit.

Get professional help if:

- Individual cannot talk, eat, or lie flat in bed to sleep.
- Temperature over 101° several times in one day.
- Sputum changes from clear white to yellow, green, gray, or red.
- Vomiting occurs more than twice in a few hours (especially children).

BLADDER INFECTION

What you need to know:

Description: An infection of the bladder and urethra that in some cases spreads up to ureters and kidneys.

● Properly and promptly treated, this disease is self-limiting: it runs its course in three days.

● Usually caused by bacteria, but sometimes a virus is at fault.

● More common in women who do not wipe from *front* to back and who use bubble bath products.

Home care supplies:

thermometer   aspirin
glasses of water   cranberry juice

SOAP Selfcare Symptoms

1 Subjective:

- back/lower abdominal pain
- bed wetting/night urination
- blood in urine
- burning urination
- change in odor, color of urine
- chills/fever; sweating
- frequent urination
- pain over pubic area

2 Objective:

- Note temperature three times daily.
- Punch kidney areas of back very gently on each side. Is there pain? If so, suspect kidney infection and call doctor.
- Record color of urine.

3 **Assessment:**

- How many subjective conditions are present? _____
- How many objective findings are present? _____

4 **Plan:**

- Increase liquid intake to replace lost fluids; drink 8 oz. of water or juice every *hour.*
- If feverish, rest in bed to conserve energy and shorten illness.
- Take aspirin for pain—especially useful at bedtime.
- Take hot sitz baths in tub (one-fourth filled with warm water) to relieve burning (see p. 161).
- Avoid alcohol, tea, coffee, which are urinary tract irritants.

Get professional help if:

- Diabetic
- History of kidney disease
- Blood in urine (hematuria) persists for 24 hours
- Pregnant
- Symptoms persist after 24 hours of home treatment

What you need to know:

Description: Life-threatening condition that results from blocked airway or cardiac arrest.

● The basic steps in a breathing emergency (the A-B-Cs of cardiopulmonary resuscitation) are:
Airway→Breathing→Circulation.

● Do not attempt neck lift with suspected neck fracture.

Home care supplies:

syringe   plastic airway

SOAP Selfcare System

1 Place patient on back. Put your ear close to patient's mouth to detect breathing. Clean out mouth with syringe. Insert plastic airway.

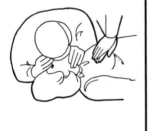

2 If patient is not breathing, raise neck with one hand; push forehead down with other hand. If patient does not start breathing, pinch nostrils shut and blow air into mouth. When chest moves up, take your mouth away and let chest go down. Do four quick, full breaths without allowing time for patient's lungs to fully deflate. For infants and children, cover both mouth and nose with your mouth; use smaller breaths once every three seconds.

3 If cardiac arrest occurs, apply pressure rhythmically over lower half of chest plate. Alternate with emergency breathing.

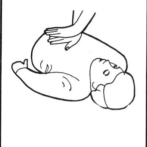

4 If there is one rescuer, perform both breathing and circulation with a 15 to 2 ratio (after 15 chest compressions at a rate of 80/minute, two very quick lung inflations). If two rescuers, perform both breathing and circulation with a 5 to 2 ratio (after five chest compressions at a rate of 60/minute, two lung inflations). For infants and children, do the same with less force and faster compression rate (80 to 100/minute).

Get professional help if:

● Breathing, heartbeat, and pulse do not resume after you follow the treatment above several times.

BRONCHIAL INFECTION

What you need to know:

Description: Infection of the airways (bronchial tubes) caused by bacteria or viruses.
● Chronic bronchitis can lead to serious chronic obstructive lung disease, if untreated.
● Bronchitis is contagious; take precautions to isolate patient.
● Typically, it is preceded by an upper respiratory infection.

Home care supplies:

thermometer   glasses of water
stethoscope   cold air vaporizer
watch with second hand   cough medicine

SOAP Selfcare System

1 Subjective:
- ● aches or chest pain (adults)
- ● bad breath
- ● chills/fever; sweating
- ● coughing or coughing up blood
- ● hoarseness; sore throat
- ● runny nose
- ● wheezing

2 Objective:
- ● Note temperature three times daily.
- ● Note color of sputum during the day (NOT IN THE MORNING). Yellow, green, or brown indicates a bacterial infection, which may require an antibiotic.

3 Assessment:
- How many subjective conditions are present? _____
- How many objective findings are present? _____

4 Plan:
- Rest. Go to bed if feverish.
- Drink liquids—aim for one 8-oz. glass every hour.
- Humidify air with cold vapor.
- Use postural drainage technique twice daily (see illustration).
- Take cough medicine, especially at night.
- Massage chest and back muscles to increase blood flow.
- Stop smoking (and never start again).

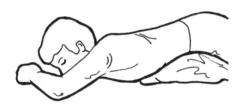

Get professional help if:

- History of chronic lung disease or bronchitis.
- Cough persists.
- Over 60 years old.
- Pulse over 100 beats/minute.
- Temperature over 101° several times in one day.
- Respiration rate over 20-25/minute, 40 for infants.

What you need to know:

Description: A blistering burn resulting from heat, chemicals, or radiation.

● Second-degree burns occur when tissue injury allows blood plasma to leak out of blood vessels into surrounding tissue and forms a blister.

● Burns are more serious for the young and old because they disturb fluid balance.

Home care supplies:

tape
gauze dressing or cloth strips
ice

burn ointment or
    petroleum jelly

SOAP Selfcare System

1 Does burn cover more than 10% of body surface? If so, this causes shifts in body fluids, which may require hospitalization. Such extensive burns should not be covered with dressings or oil-based substances.

2 If less than 10% of body burned, apply cold water or ice to burn area (see p. 162) for *one hour,* washing with mild soap.

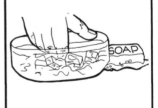

3 Apply oil-based substance (medicated ointment or petroleum jelly). Cover with sterile gauze bandage or strips of clean cloth. Tape dressing loosely in place. Elevate burned area to help drainage. Keep it motionless to facilitate healing. Bed rest may be needed when feet or lower legs are burned.

4 Keep dressings on for one week unless they become soaked with plasma or develop an unpleasant odor. In that case, change them. To remove dressing, rinse with lots of cold water.

Get professional help if:

- Burn covers more than 10% of body surface.
- Areas of brown or blackened skin (third-degree burn) are evident.
- Under 14 or over 64 years old.
- Persistent pain is not relieved by aspirin.

What you need to know:

Description: Pain in chest that radiates into left arm, often with nausea, clammy skin, irregular heartbeat.

● About 90% of suspected cases of chest pain are not due to heart attack but to a wide variety of musculo-skeletal, gastrointestinal, emotional, and pulmonary causes.

● The first few hours are most critical in dealing with heart attacks, yet the classic signs are present in only 60-70% of the cases. If the heart attack is real, you can tell with the self-test below.

Self-Test for Chest Pain

The following questions are designed to determine the odds that your chest pain is really a sign of a heart attack. *No* answers will indicate other causes of your chest pain. If you answer yes to most questions, CALL FOR HELP.

1. Place tip of index finger over center of chest pain; estimate distance (in inches) from centerline of chest. Is fingertip *2″ or less* from line? (If yes, go to Step 2.)
2. Is the pain *above or even* with the nipple line? (If yes, go to Step 3.)
3. Is the pain *between* nipple and centerline? (If yes, go to Step 4.)
4. Is there pain on the *right side* of the chest? (If yes, go to Step 5.)
5. Can discomfort be described as a *dull pressure* or squeezing sensation under the necktie area? (If yes, go to Step 6.)
6. Is pain *continuous* (not coming and going)? (If yes, go to Step 7.)
7. Does discomfort last *at least* 5 to 10 minutes? (If yes, go to Step 8.)
8. Does pain *radiate* out to the arms, neck, jaws, or any combination thereof? (If yes, go to Step 9.)
9. Is the discomfort *inside* of the arm? (If yes, go to Step 10.)
   Note: To further evaluate arm discomfort, raise your arm over your head. If painful, stop. This type of pain is most likely caused by bursitis or shoulder arthritis.
10. Is there *sweating* with the pain? (If yes, go to Step 11.)
11. Is discomfort worse while *lying down?* (If yes, go to Step 12.)
12. If you've answered yes to most of the above questions, CALL FOR PROFESSIONAL HELP. It is quite likely that you need further study.

This test was originally designed as a telephone screening quiz by Glenn O. Turner, M.D.

Chest Pain Chart

The most common conditions that can cause chest pain are noted below, with a description of the characteristics of the pain and any associated symptoms.

	Heart Pain (Angina)	Gall Bladder Spasm	Stomach (Hiatal) Hernia	Anxiety
Pain Location	Chest midline; may spread across chest.	Upper abdomen; may spread to chest midline.	Upper abdomen and chest; often no symptoms.	Variable or over left chest.
Extent of Pain	Arms, neck, jaw; any combination of them.	Lower ribs to back, beneath right shoulder, left region and shoulder.	Arms, neck, jaw, or combinations of them.	Generally none.
Length of Pain	Usually 1-5 min.	Usually constant for hours; intermittent colic sometimes.	2 min.-1 hour.	Less than 1 min. to a few hours.
Type of Pain	Heavy pressure or discomfort.	Severe, rapidly intensifying pain.	Dull discomfort.	Discomfort or sharp, stabbing pain.
Related Symptoms	Indigestion	Upper abdominal discomfort, nausea, vomiting, bloating, belching, dark urine.	Heartburn, hiccups, belching.	Jitters, worries, nervous stomach.
Causes	Exertion, emotion, foods, cold.	Large meals, fried foods.	Bending over, lying down, heavy meals.	Fatigue, emotion, stress.
Relief	Stop effort, take medicine.	Drink liquids, watch diet.	Drink liquids, sit or stand upright, take antacids.	Lie down, manage stress better, take medications.

Home care supplies

blood pressure unit   thermometer
stethoscope   watch with second hand

SOAP Selfcare System

1 Subjective:
Musculo-skeletal causes
● Chest wall aching worsened by deep breathing or twisting movement of upper body.
● Localized tenderness over ribs following history of fall or chest trauma.
● Neck pain worsened by movement of head and neck. May also produce aching in chest or upper arm.

Gastrointestinal causes
● Tenderness of abdomen at centerline (imaginary line from belly button to Adam's apple) under ribs, with related burning in stomach.
● Intermittent pain in upper abdomen on right, occasionally radiating to back under right shoulder blade (gall bladder problems).
● Burning pain at centerline, under ribs, that radiates to the jaws. Worsened by lying flat (esophagitis). Often occurs in obese people.

Emotional causes
● Chest pain associated with anxiety or stressful conditions.
● Chest pain related to hyperventilation (excessive rate and depth of respiration, causing abnormal loss of carbon dioxide from blood), due to emotional upset.

Pulmonary causes
● Chest pain in young adults or adults who have asthma or chronic obstructive pulmonary disease.
● Sudden shortness of breath, apprehension, sweating, and faintness in people with history of phlebitis (inflammation of veins in legs) or calf pain, or while legs are immobilized for surgery or other reasons.

2 **Objective:**

- Take Self-Test for Chest Pain (p. 185).
- Take blood pressure and record.
- Check pulse and record.
- Note breathing rate and record.
- Take temperature and record.

3 **Plan:**

- If pain has persisted for more than 15 minutes, ask someone to take you to the nearest hospital. If no one can help you, call the rescue squad.
- Lie down and rest. Do not drive the car yourself!
- Tell the emergency room attendant you may be having a heart attack and insist on going to the coronary care unit—even if you only suspect a heart attack!

Get professional help if:

- Your answers for the Self-Test are *yes.* Immediately CALL THE RESCUE SQUAD and get to a hospital. (Transfer later on to a coronary unit may be needed.)
- Your chest pain has persisted for 15 minutes.

CHOKING

What you need to know:

Description: Obstruction of the airway caused by object or food lodged in passage.

● Look for these three signals: bluish face and lips, complete collapse, and inability to speak.

● You can learn more about the Heimlich hug in CPR courses.

SOAP Selfcare System

1 For standing patient, stand behind and wrap your arms around patient's waist. Make a fist, and use other hand to grab it. Place against patient's abdomen, slightly above navel and below rib cage. Press into abdomen with quick upward thrust. Repeat if necessary.

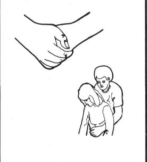

2 For patient lying down on back, kneel astride patient's hips, facing patient. Put one hand on top of the other; apply heel or bottom hand on abdomen above navel and below rib cage. Press into abdomen with quick upward thrust.

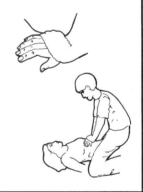

3 If you are alone, apply force just below your abdomen by pressing into a table, chair, or sink, or by using your own fist.

4 For child, turn child upside down over one arm in a jackknife position. Apply blows to the back between shoulder blades.

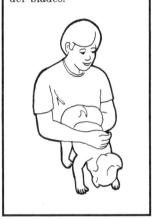

Get professional help if:

● Choking occurs. Have someone else CALL RESCUE SQUAD for assistance while you begin above procedure.

COMMON COLD

What you need to know:

Description: A virus-caused inflammation of nasal and throat membranes; frequently involves ears and chest.
- Colds last three to seven days.
- Symptoms usually subside after third day.
- Antibiotics such as penicillin or tetracycline have no value in treating colds and may make them worse by creating resistant bacteria strains and/or diarrhea or stomach upset.

Home care supplies:

thermometer
spoon handle as tongue
  depressor
hot saltwater gargles
nose drops

aspirin
penlight
glasses of water
nasal aspirator

SOAP Selfcare System

1 Subjective:
- bad breath
- breathing problems
- chills/fever
- congested or runny nose
- ear, neck, headaches
- postnasal drip, sneezing
- sore throat

2 Objective:
- Check temperature three times daily.
- Look down throat and record findings.
- Check number and location of enlarged lymph nodes.

3 **Assessment:**

- How many subjective conditions are present? _____
- How many objective findings are present? _____

4 **Plan:**

- Drink 8 oz. of water or juice each hour.
- Eat chicken soup—it actually has decongestant and curative properties!
- Gargle with hot saltwater every two hours to relieve throat pain and clear mucus (see p. 160).
- Draw mucus from nose of infants with nasal aspirator.
- Apply nose drops twice daily.
- Take aspirin for pain or fever.
- Use throat lozenges for sore throat.
- Wash hands and face frequently to prevent infecting others.
- Rest. Go to bed if fever exists.
- Increase Vitamin C intake.

Get professional help if:

- Temperature over 101° several times in one day.
- Earache, sinus pain, or chest pain develops.
- Coughing produces green or gray sputum.
- White or yellow spots on tonsils or throat.
- No improvement after four days.

CONVULSION (FIT, SEIZURE)

What you need to know:

Description: Involuntary twitching and tremors of muscle groups followed by period of unconsciousness.

● Convulsions are most common in children with high fevers.

● Unconsciousness may range from a few moments of confusion to deep sleep.

● Convulsions, in themselves, rarely cause death; main hazards are injuries to head during seizure.

Home care supplies:

pen and paper   safety or straight pin

SOAP Selfcare System

1 Subjective:
- biting tongue
- blacking out
- breathing trouble
- chills/fever
- "funny feeling" before or after
- heart palpitations
- headache; stiff neck
- nausea, vomiting

2 Objective:
- During convulsion, check airway (open the airway if necessary—see p. 178). Only put fingers in mouth with extreme caution.
- Remove objects the person might hit.
- Gently restrain the person (no need to grasp tongue).

3 **Assessment:**

- How many subjective conditions are present? _____
- How many objective findings are present? _____

4 **Plan:**

- DO NOT MOVE person unless necessary for safety. DO NOT put fingers in mouth.
- Loosen collar and tight clothing. Turn person on side.
- Check airway and skin color.
- Examine personal effects for medical card or ID tag showing history of epilepsy.
- Write down information gathered on paper, and pin to person or give to rescue squad.

Get professional help if:

- A convulsion of any kind occurs in adults or children. CALL RESCUE SQUAD for assistance and transportation.

What you need to know:

Description: Any break in skin, such as an abrasion, laceration, puncture, or cut.

- When injury occurs, don't panic; this increases heart rate and speeds loss of blood. KEEP CALM.
- Over 50% of all cuts or wounds can be handled safely without professional help.

Home care supplies:

gauze dressings
ice cubes
plastic bag

antibacterial ointment
soap and water

SOAP Selfcare System

1 If bleeding, apply *direct pressure* to wound with clean cloth. Continue pressure for three minutes.

2 If bleeding is not profuse, apply ice in plastic bag to minimize swelling. Wash wound if dirty, making sure particles are flushed out.

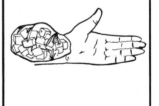

3 Apply antibacterial ointment. If necessary, use butterfly closures to pull edges together (see p. 164). Dress wound.

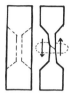

4 If cut is on finger or toe, tape to adjacent digit. If elsewhere, use tape or splint to keep injured area immobile. Change dressing daily.

Get professional help if:

- Deep wound longer than 1 inch.
- Bleeding or pain persists.
- Caused by human or animal bite.
- Last tetanus shot was 5 years ago (after a contaminated wound) or 10 years ago (after a clean wound).
- Wound is "dirty" (occurring outdoors).

What you need to know:

Description: An inflammation of the middle ear, usually caused by bacterial infection.

● Otitis media is most common in children and adolescents but may be found in people of all ages.

● Colds often cause eustachian tubes to swell and close.

● Bacterial infections of middle ear in children under three years old may be painless (thus unnoticed) and child may tug or rub ear(s).

Home care supplies:

otoscope	hot water bottle
nose drops	or heating pad
Debrox ear drops	thermometer

SOAP Selfcare System

1 Subjective:
- ● aching/pain/sound in ear
- ● chills/fever
- ● congestion, runny nose
- ● dizziness
- ● ear discharge
- ● fussing/tugging ear (child)
- ● headache
- ● hearing loss

2 Objective:
- ● Check temperature three times daily.
- ● Look at eardrum.

3 **Assessment:**

- How many subjective conditions are present? _____
- How many objective findings are present? _____

4 **Plan:**

- Apply nose drops *immediately;* sniff two to three drops in nostril on same side as earache. Turn head with "bad ear" down after application.
- If eardrum appears black or brown, clean dark wax out by using Debrox.
- Say "K-K-K" for one minute after dosing to draw the nose drops into the back of nose, near the eustachian tube.
- Apply heat to ear (see p. 159-160).
- Rest; go to bed if there is fever.

Get professional help if:

- Patient is under three years old.
- Pain increases despite treatment.
- Dizziness develops.
- Temperature is over 102°.
- Eardrum ruptures. Look for yellow to reddish fluid draining from ear.

What you need to know:

Description: Blow to fingertip causing intense pain, swelling, and black-and-blue fingernail.

● Over 90% of fingertip injuries can be treated at home.

● When fingertip receives hard blow the nail turns black and blue in several hours. Intense pain comes from accumulated blood trapped between nail and bone. Releasing the blood reduces the pain.

Home care supplies:

ice
sharp blade or penknife

cloth or gauze
bandage (gauze type)

SOAP Selfcare System

1 Apply ice or cold water as soon as possible to reduce swelling (see p. 162).

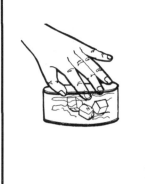

2 Have assistant hold finger or stabilize it yourself. Drill hole in nail using point of sharp blade. (Or use hot tip of paper clip.)

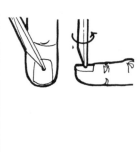

3 When hole is through nail, place tip of gauze or cloth into hole to absorb blood. Pain should be relieved immediately.

4 Cover hole with a gauze-type (not Telfa) bandage so blood continues to drain. Keep nail covered for a few days.

Get professional help if:

- Bony deformity suggests fracture or dislocation.
- Inability to straighten finger suggests damage to tendon.
- Drilling impossible—patient uncooperative, patient alone, or tip badly swollen.
- Pain persists after drilling.

What you need to know:

Description: Foreign particles, chips, or other materials lodged in sensitive eye tissue.
- Do not rub or further irritate eye after injury.
- Normal tearing will occur immediately—tears may wash out the particle.

Home care supplies:

penlight   water to wash out eye
handkerchief   matchstick

SOAP Selfcare System

1 Wash out eye with cold water. Face assistant, looking in opposite direction while assistant locates object. Touch with corner of handkerchief.

2 If object is beneath upper lid, have assistant grasp its lashes between thumb and index finger; while patient is looking *down,* pull upper lid over *lower* lid.

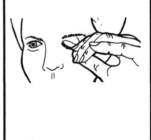

3 Another way to remove objects under upper lid is to "flip" the eyelid with a matchstick.

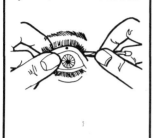

4 After object is removed, DO NOT RUB EYE; it will be sensitive for several hours. Reduce visual activities for 24 hours; avoid bright light or sunlight without sunglasses.

Get professional help if:

- Foreign object was impelled at high speed.
- History of previous injury with scarring of cornea.
- Foreign object cannot be removed in two or three attempts.
- Patient has only one good eye and foreign body is in that eye.

FOREIGN OBJECT IN LIMB

What you need to know:

Description: Foreign objects such as splinters, thorns, fish-hooks, or glass slivers embedded in tissue.
● Most objects close to skin surface are easily removed.

Home care supplies:

soap and water
ice
Band-Aid

large sewing needle or
tweezers

SOAP Selfcare System

1 Before attempting extraction, scrub skin carefully with soap and water. Sterilize tweezers and needle over flame or in boiling water.

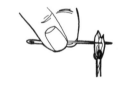

2 Locate object. Numb area with ice cube. With point of needle, slightly enlarge wound to make extraction easier.

3 Flick out splinter or particle with needle or grasp it with tweezers. If object is fishhook, expose and clip barb as below and pull back through.

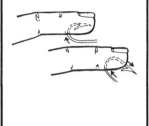

4 After extraction, cleanse again with soap and water. Cover with Band-Aid. If finger or toe is affected, tape it to adjacent digit. Use splint to immobilize other areas (see p. 165). Soak puncture site in hot water for 20-30 minutes twice daily for one week. Change dressing daily for one week. (See p. 164).

Get professional help if:

- Object is deeply imbedded.
- Affected area shows swelling or red streaks, or lymph nodes are swollen two to three days after injury.
- Booster shot for tetanus is needed (should have booster every 10 years after third initial injection or after clean wound, and five years after contaminated wound).

HIGH BLOOD PRESSURE

What you need to know:

Description: Elevation of blood pressure above usually normal limits.

● Hypertension has been called the "silent disease" because it may exist for years without apparent symptoms.

● Normal blood pressure is 130/80 or less. At 150/90, regardless of age, treatment is considered.

Home care supplies:

blood pressure unit   stethoscope
  (electronic or aneroid)

SOAP Selfcare System

1 Subjective:
- blackout spells; dizziness
- blurred or lost vision
- fatigue, depression
- headache
- insomnia, irritability
- numbness of lips, face, arms
- paralysis/weakness/twitching

2 Objective:
- Check blood pressure weekly.
- Check body weight and calculate ideal weight according to height. (Female: 100 + 5 lbs. for each inch over 60 inches. Male: 106 + 6 lbs. for each inch over 60 inches.)

3 **Assessment:**

- How many subjective conditions are present? _____
- How many objective findings are present? _____

4 **Plan:**

- Lose weight if 20% over "ideal weight."
- Cut down salt in diet.
- Stop smoking.
- Avoid coffee, tea, and cola drinks; caffeine elevates blood pressure.
- Maintain regular, vigorous exercise for 20 minutes, three times a week.
- If on medication for hypertension, take as prescribed.
- Learn to control or cope with stress.
- Take regular vacations and use weekends wisely for rest and recreation.

Get professional help if:

- Unexplained numbness of lips, face, or arms occurs.
- Heart palpitations, skipped beats, or shortness of breath occurs.
- Reaction to blood pressure medication is suspected, such as weakness, blurred vision, depression, fatigue, constipation, dizziness.

INSECT BITE/STING

What you need to know:

Description: Pain and reaction to venom that follows insect bite or sting of wasp, bee, or hornet.

● A few people (about 4%) experience a severe allergic reaction to stings. Left untreated, it can be fatal.

● Usually the pain and welt will subside in three to four hours.

● Keeping calm will keep the venom from spreading suddenly and triggering a reaction.

Home care supplies:

Adolph's Meat Tenderizer   ice
aspirin   baking soda
clean cloth or gauze   household ammonia

SOAP Selfcare System

1 In an allergic reaction, stop spread of venom by firmly gripping area or applying pressure with a tourniquet-like wrapping between site and heart. Get professional help.

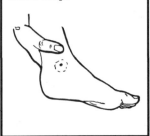

2 If no allergic reaction, remove stinger by scraping with fingernail or knife blade (don't use tweezers). Then wash area.

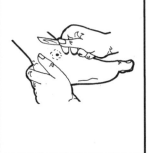

3 Put meat tenderizer on wet cloth or gauze. Place on sting for 20-30 minutes. Or apply ice or cold compresses (see p. 163).

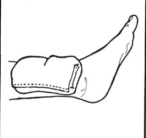

4 If itching or pain persists, apply baking soda/ammonia (one-half cup soda with enough ammonia to make a paste) to skin. Take aspirin for pain. For next two to three days, try to avoid sweating, which may renew irritation.

Get professional help if:

- Evidence of severe allergic reaction: swelling, itching eyes or lips; shortness of breath, wheezing; clammy, bluish skin; abdominal cramps, nausea.
- Family history of allergic reactions to stings.
- Known allergies.
- Multiple stings.

NOSEBLEED

What you need to know:

Description: Bleeding from nose caused by injury, common cold, allergies, dry climate, or cracked, infected mucous surface.

● The direct pressure method (below) will control 90% of bleeding from nose.

● No matter what the cause, blood from nose nearly always comes from front part of nose, not head or lungs.

Home care supplies:

Vaseline

SOAP Selfcare System

1 Squeeze nostrils firmly enough to stop bleeding without causing pain. (Gentle pressure may be applied to nose even if bones are broken.)

2 Lean trunk forward, still applying direct pressure. Do not lie down.

3 Continue applying pressure for full *five minutes.* Relax. If bleeding recurs, continue pressure for five more minutes.

4 When bleeding is stopped, remain quiet for two to three hours. On third day after nosebleed, apply Vaseline inside nostrils twice daily.

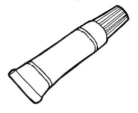

Get professional help if:

- Bleeding is not controlled after repeating methods above three times.
- Difficulty in breathing.
- Taking anticoagulants.
- Nose has been broken.
- History of bleeding problems, blood disorders, or high blood pressure.

PINK EYE

What you need to know:

Description: Inflammation of mucous covering of eye and eyelid, characterized by pink or bright red streaks.
● Conjunctivitis is contagious.
● Serious eye conditions such as acute iritis, acute narrowangle glaucoma, and herpes simplex may cause similar symptoms.
● If pink eye occurs six to eight hours after chipping paint or using grinding wheel, look for a tiny sliver of metal lodged in eye (see p. 200).

Home care supplies:

aspirin   sunglasses
white handkerchief   penlight
eyedrops

SOAP Selfcare System

1 Subjective:
  ● blurred or decreased vision
  ● headache
  ● itchy, red, or watery eyes
  ● matter (mucus) in eyes
  ● swollen eyelids
  ● sticky eyelids that matter shut after sleep

2 Objective:
  ● Check for sandy, scratchy discomfort.
  ● Look for sticky mucus by touching eye with corner of clean, white handkerchief.
  ● Note any difference in size of pupils. A constricted pupil may indicate iritis (see above).

3 **Assessment:**
- How many subjective conditions are present? _____
- How many objective findings are present? _____

4 **Plan:**
- Apply warm, wet compresses to eyes four times a day for 10 minutes (see p. 160).
- Avoid wiping eyes.
- Take aspirin
- Wear protective sunglasses
- Get doctor's approval for use of prior prescription for eye drops
- DO NOT USE EYE DROPS CONTAINING CORTISONE PREPARATIONS.

Get professional help if:

- Distinct pain in eye itself or radiating to temple is felt.
- Vision changes or returning to well-lighted area after prolonged darkness (driving at night or after a movie) causes pain.
- Change in ability to see or in pupil size.
- No improvement after 24 hours.

POISONING

What you need to know:

Description: Life-threatening condition caused by ingestion of harmful solids, liquids, or gases.

● Children under five are especially susceptible to poisoning; they may taste medicines, cleaning products, chemicals, or plants.

● Industrial or occupational exposure, accidental ingestion, suicide attempts, and other factors cause adult poisoning.

Home care supplies:

penlight   syrup of ipecac (for child)

SOAP Selfcare System

1 Subjective:
- abdominal pain; diarrhea
- blackout, unconsciousness
- blurred vision; convulsions
- choking, trouble breathing
- confusion, drowsiness
- coughing up blood; nausea
- dizziness, behavior change
- rash, burn

2 Objective:
- Check victim's breath for odors.
- Note significant objects near victim.
- Check lips and mouth for caustic burns.
- Shine penlight at pupil; if it doesn't constrict, suspect poisoning.
- Obtain sample of vomitus.

3 Assessment:
- How many subjective conditions are present? _____
- How many objective findings are present? _____

4 Plan:
- CALL POISON CONTROL CENTER.
- Open windows and doors *quickly* if in closed room.
- Clear airway; do emergency breathing if necessary (see p. 178).
- If toxic substance is ingested by mouth and container is found, *administer antidote* according to label.
- Induce vomiting (EXCEPT for caustic lyes, or if victim is unconscious or having convulsions). Use finger in throat for adults, syrup of ipecac for children.

Get professional help if:

- Poisoning of any kind occurs.
- CALL RESCUE SQUAD for assistance and transportation if victim is seriously ill.
- CALL POISON CONTROL CENTER for information and assistance.

What you need to know:

Description: Emotional crisis associated with alcohol or drug abuse, depression, or acute psychiatric conditions.
● Most common psychiatric emergency is "difficult drunk" or person experiencing hallucinations or delusions and violent paranoia. Both alcohol and mind-changing drugs can cause delirium.
● Other emergencies are severe depression, manic states, and acute schizophrenic breakdown.

Home care supplies:

SOAP Selfcare System

1 **Subjective:**
● Because of unknown factors surrounding psychiatric emergencies, information about symptoms is not universally reliable.
● Alcohol/chemical abuse—alcoholics can become disoriented and visual or auditory hallucinations may accompany or precede DTs (delirium tremens).
● Drugs—psychedelic drugs may produce sensory aberrations and confusion.
● Depression—symptoms include insomnia, headache, fatigue, diminished sex drive, loss of appetite.

2 **Plan:**

- Schizophrenia—contact a trained professional, as patient can be dangerous if armed with firearms or weapons.
- Violent behavior—a person who goes berserk may need to be restrained for safety's sake. A good rule of thumb is "4 for 1," that is, four people to restrain one.
- Depression—if suicide is attempted or threatened, try to keep the person talking while awaiting aid.
- Lesser psychiatric emergencies—seek help from a qualified professional.

Get professional help if:

- Person seems dangerous (carrying firearms or weapons) or is unconscious or unresponsive to stimuli (questions, sounds). CALL RESCUE SQUAD for assistance and transportation.

SCIATICA/BACK PAIN

What you need to know:

Description: A common back disorder in which pain radiates down the back of the leg.
● When semicartilaginous "shock absorber" located between bony vertebrae deteriorates or is injured, pain may result.
● Inferior level of fitness or neglect of spinal flexibility exercises may lead to sciatica.

Home care supplies:

pillows
firm mattress

kitchen-type chair
aspirin

SOAP Selfcare System

1 Take prompt preventive action. Change position; adjust car seat; avoid low chairs; be sure to lift properly.

2 If pain or distress persists despite prompt protective action, intravertebral disc may have already protruded enough to irritate sciatic nerve.

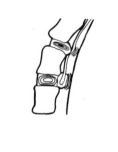

3   Perform hyperextension: lie face down with two pillows under chest. Or lean with hands against surface; bend back and head backward.

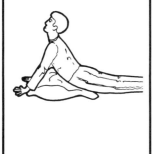

4   During the next two to three days: Do moderate work, but no lifting. Maintain proper sitting and standing posture. Do hyperextension exercise three times a day. Rest for 20 minutes each noon, lying flat on floor or firm mattress. Sit only on kitchen-type chairs. Take aspirin for pain.

Get professional help if:

- Numbness in leg persists.
- History of repeated sciatica attacks.
- Pain remains after treatment plan.

SHOCK

What you need to know:

Description: Life-threatening depression of vital body functions caused by injury, infection, heart attack, poisoning.

● Degree of shock may be altered by age, body temperature, general health, reaction to stress or pain, handling of patient and treatment.

● Always seek professional help as quickly as possible.

Home care supplies:

blankets or heavy coats   watch with second hand
blood pressure unit

SOAP Selfcare System

1 Subjective:
- ● bluish skin
- ● chills, shaking, shivering
- ● dizziness, unconsciousness
- ● moist, clammy skin
- ● nausea, vomiting
- ● numbness, pain
- ● thirst
- ● trouble breathing

2 Objective:
- ● Check skin/mucous linings of mouth for color: pale or bluish?
- ● Check skin: is it moist?
- ● Check pulse at wrist or angle of jaw: is rate over 100/minute? weak or steady?
- ● Check blood pressure: less than 100/60?

3 **Assessment:**
- How many subjective conditions are present? _____
- How many objective findings are present? _____

4 **Plan:**
- Clear airway.
- DO NOT MOVE patient unless necessary for safety.
- Loosen collar and tight clothing and turn patient on side.
- Cover patient lightly.
- Keep patient *lying down;* elevate legs 10″-12″ on blankets or pillows.

Get professional help if:

- Person goes into shock. CALL RESCUE SQUAD for assistance and transportation.

SHOULDER OR ELBOW PAIN

What you need to know:

Description: Soft-tissue injury to shoulder or elbow joint caused by overuse.

● Rather than the specific sport or action, it is the *motion* involved with twisting or lifting that causes pain and limitations of joint.

● Cause may be improper conditioning or neglected warm-ups.

Home care supplies:

Cold Comfort (3M)   triangle sling
aspirin

SOAP Selfcare System

1 Subjective:

- ● ache/pain in shoulder, elbow
- ● limited motion of joint
- ● sleep loss due to pain
- ● stiffness
- ● swelling in joint

2 Objective:

- ● Check joint for swelling (which may be extensive) and fluid accumulation.
- ● Note events leading to attack and motions that aggravate condition.

3 Assessment:
- How many subjective conditions are present? ____
- How many objective findings are present? ____

4 Plan:
Immediate treatment plan:
- Apply cold for first 24 hours, three times a day for 10-15 minutes (see p. 162).
- Apply heat for next 48 hours, three times a day for 10-15 minutes (see p. 159).
- Take aspirin for pain.
- Use triangle sling.

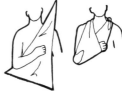

Follow-up treatment plan:
- Gently massage muscles.

Get professional help if:

- Joint is swollen; it may require tapping and fluid drainage.
- Pain persists after two to three days of home treatment.
- History of previous attacks of bursitis or tendonitis.

What you need to know:

Description: Inflammation and infection of sinus cavities in cheekbones and forehead.
● Maxillary (cheekbone) sinusitis is most common form of sinus infection.
● About 50% of sinus infections are bacterial and are helped by antibiotics.

Home care supplies:

thermometer   glasses of water
nose drops   hot/cold compresses and pans
hot saltwater gargles

Soap Selfcare System

1 Subjective:
- ● bad breath
- ● bloody nose
- ● blurred vision, headache
- ● chills/fever
- ● postnasal drainage
- ● runny or congested nose
- ● tenderness over forehead, cheek

2 Objective:
- ● Note temperature three times daily.
- ● Is headache worse when bending over to touch toes?
- ● Gently blow nose and examine discharge. Is it yellow or streaked with blood?

3 Assessment:

- How many subjective conditions are present? _____
- How many objective findings are present? _____

4 Plan:

- At first sign of distress, use alternating hot and cold compresses over face twice daily. Apply each for 5-10 minutes (see pp. 159-163).
- Apply nose drops after using compresses. Sniff two to three drops into each nostril. Say "K-K-K" for one minute.
- Gargle to clear out mucus (see p. 160)
- Increase fluid intake.
- Stop smoking.
- Rest; go to bed if feverish.

Get professional help if:

- Temperature over 101° several times a day.
- Bleeding from nose.
- Blurring or change in vision.
- Increased thick nasal discharge.
- Increased swelling of forehead, eye area, sides of nose, cheeks.

SORE THROAT

What you need to know:

Description: Inflammation of throat caused by viral or bacterial infection.
● Over 80% of sore throats are caused by viruses and are not helped by antibiotics.
● Main complication is "strep" infection caused by Group A, betahemolytic streptococcus bacteria. It can only be determined by throat culture.

Home care supplies:

thermometer
spoon handle as tongue
  depressor
penlight
hot salt water

hot liquids
glasses of water
aspirin
lozenges

SOAP Selfcare System

1 Subjective:
- bad breath
- chills/fever
- headaches, neck aches
- hoarseness
- lymph nodes in neck enlarged or tender
- runny or congested nose
- sore throat

2 Objective:
- Check temperature three times daily and record.
- Check throat color.
- Count swollen lymph nodes of neck; note location.

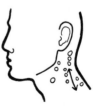

3 Assessment:

- How many subjective conditions are present? _____
- How many objective findings are present? _____

4 Plan:

- Gargle with hot saltwater every two hours to relieve pain and clear mucus (see p. 160).
- Take frequent sips of hot liquids such as lemonade or weak tea
- Drink an 8-oz. glass of water or juice each hour to replace lost fluids.
- Take aspirin for pain or fever.
- Use throat lozenges to soothe rawness.
- Wash hands and face frequently to limit spread of infection.
- Stop smoking (and don't start again).
- Rest; go to bed if fever exists.

Get professional help if:

- Sore throat persists for five days.
- Fever over 101° several times a day.
- Rash develops.
- History of rheumatic fever, kidney disease, or frequent strep infection.

SPRAINED ANKLE

What you need to know:

Description: Damage to ligaments or joint capsule of ankle following a twisting fall.

● Sprained ankles tend to be underdiagnosed and undertreated, which can lead to lifelong disability—limping, unstable ankle; swollen ankle; foot pain; or difficulty on rough terrain.

● Severity of sprain often has no relation to severity of complications.

Home care supplies:

ice

pillows

elastic bandage

crutches

SOAP Selfcare System

1 Follow these steps as needed, with professional's advice. Apply ice or cold compress (see p. 162) for one hour.

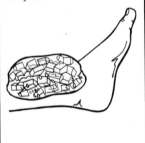

2 Immobilize ankle by elevating on two to three pillows for 24 hours. Wrap firmly with elastic bandage to control swelling (see p. 163).

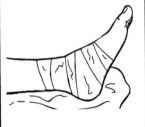

3 There are two methods of sprain treatment; physician will choose best method. *Non-weight-bearing*—wrap in elastic bandage, use crutches and stay off foot for one week (mild sprain) or two weeks (severe sprain). *Early weight-bearing*—apply cast or basketweave tape splint (see p. 165) Use crutches for three weeks.

4 If elastic bandage is used, remove twice a day for hot soak and ankle massage. Later wear ankle-supporting boots.

Get professional help if:

• Ankle is at an abnormal angle. Because of difficulties in evaluating ankle injuries, most sprains should be seen by physician.

STOMACH FLU (GASTROENTERITUS)

What you need to know:

Description: Disorder of digestive system with nausea, vomiting, diarrhea.

● About 90% of gastroenteritis cases are caused by viruses and run their course in 24-48 hours.

● Diarrhea may be PROTECTIVE, as the body speeds offending particles through digestive tract. So don't take antidiarrheal medication during first six to eight hours.

Home care supplies:

thermometer	soft foods
ice chips	clear liquids (tea, broth)

SOAP Selfcare System

1 Subjective:
- ● abdominal pain, stomachache
- ● chills/fever
- ● diarrhea
- ● dry mouth
- ● headache
- ● muscle aches
- ● nausea, vomiting

2 Objective:
- ● Note temperature three times daily.
- ● Note location and pattern of pain, if present.
- ● Record number and kind of stools.
- ● Is anyone who ate the same meal sick? Has victim returned from a foreign area?

3 **Assessment:**

- How many subjective conditions are present? _____
- How many objective findings are present? _____

4 **Plan:**

- Rest in bed until nausea, vomiting, diarrhea, and fever are gone.
- Keep flat. An upright position increases amount of fluid lost during bouts of diarrhea.

Food and liquid intake:
- Day 1—ice chips only, until vomiting subsides.
- Day 2—clear liquids, sweetened tea, ginger ale, or broth.
- Day 3—soft foods, custard, baked potato, cooked cereal, pudding, Jello.
- For next five days—avoid alcohol, spicy foods, and fruits; they may bring back symptoms.

Get professional help if:

- More than eight stools or bouts of diarrhea occur per day.
- Temperature over 101° several times a day.
- Black or bloody stools, vomit.
- Infant, young child, diabetic, chronically ill, or elderly person.
- No improvement after 24 hours of home treatment.

WRIST INJURY

What you need to know:

Description: A sprain or break that occurs when wrist is bent (usually backward) beyond normal range.

● The wrist is broken more often than any other bone; true sprains are rare.

● Fractures of the wrist may involve the two bones of the forearm (ulna and radius) or the eight small carpal bones of hand and wrist.

Home care supplies:

ice   magazine/newspaper
elastic bandage   blanket or pillow

SOAP Selfcare System

1 (Follow these steps before getting professional help.) To prevent shock (see p. 218), if person feels faint, lie flat on back; elevate forearm.

2 Apply cold or ice pack or use cold, wet compresses for at least 30 minutes to minimize swelling (see p. 162).

3 Splint arm and wrist with magazine/newspaper and elastic bandage. Support arm in sling (see pp. 165, 221).

4 Check fingertips of injured arm repeatedly for swelling and bluish discoloration. If this occurs, loosen ties of splint or elastic bandage.

Get professional help if:

● Wrist injury occurs. It is important to X-ray any wrist injury to determine whether a break requires casting or other treatment. Neglect of even a hairline fracture can lead to complications in the future.
● Pain or swelling is notable or bluish discoloration visible.

Notes

pp. 15-16   "The Seven Golden Rules of Public Health"
             are summarized from the following sources:
             Lester Breslow: "A Quantitative Approach
             to the World Health Organization Definition
             of Health: Physical, Mental and Social Well-
             Being," *International Journal of Epide-
             miology* 1 (1972), no. 4; Nedra B. Belloc and
             Lester Breslow, "Relationship of Physical
             Health Status and Health Practices," *Pre-
             ventive Medicine* 1 (1972): 409-421; Nedra
             B. Belloc, "Relationship of Health Practices
             and Mortality," *Preventive Medicine* 2
             (1973): 67-81.

pp. 26-31   The "Medical Age Self-Test" is adapted
             from *How to Be Your Own Doctor, Some-
             times* by Keith W. Sehnert, M.D. with How-
             ard Eisenberg. Published by Grosset &
             Dunlap, New York.

pp. 65-66   Carl Simonton's remarks were made in a
             speech on "The Healing Power of Love and
             Laughter," delivered April 7-8, 1984 at the
             College of St. Catherine in St. Paul, Min-
             nesota.

pp. 73-74   Dr. Robert Coles' remarks were made in a
             speech at The Westminster Town Hall, Jan-
             uary 9, 1984, in Minneapolis, Minnesota.

Other Resources

Chapter 2

Cranton, Elmer M. and Brecher, Arline. *Bypassing Bypass: The New Technique of Chelation Therapy.* New York: Stein and Day, 1984.

Chapter 3

Bailey, Covert. *The-Fit-or-Fat Target Diet.* Boston: Houghton Mifflin, 1984.

Nutritional Guidelines. Publication 101, American Holistic Medical Association, Annandale VA 22003.

Chapter 4

Cousins, Norman. *The Healing Heart: Antidotes to Panic and Helplessness.* New York: W. W. Norton & Co., 1983.

Stress/Unstress Audiotapes. Augsburg Publishing House, 426 S. 5th St., Box 1209, Minneapolis MN 55440.

Chapter 5

Marty, Martin E. *Health and Medicine in the Lutheran Tradition.* New York: Crossroad Publishing Co., 1983.

Tubesing, Donald A. and Tubesing, Nancy Loving. *The Caring Question.* Minneapolis: Augsburg, 1983.

Chapter 6

Cooper, Kenneth H. *The Aerobics Way.* New York: Bantam Books, 1978.

Fixx, James F. *The Complete Book of Running.* New York: Random House, 1977.

Chapter 7
People's Medical Society Newsletter (Back copies $1), 14 E. Minor St., Emmaus PA 18049.

Chapter 8
Weil, Andrew. *Health and Healing: Understanding Conventional and Alternative Medicine.* Boston: Houghton Mifflin, 1983.

Chapter 9
Wohl, Stanley M. *The Medical Industrial Complex.* New York: Harmony Books, 1984.

Chapter 10
Medical Self-Care & SOAP Audiotapes. Sehnert Selfcare Network, 4210 Fremont Ave. S, Minneapolis MN 55409.

Ferguson, Tom. *Medical Self-Care: Access to Health Tools.* New York: Summit Books, 1980.

Index